How to Scan
A Poem

A Poetry Witch Workbook

By Annie Finch
(Scansion Assistant: Autumn Newman)

For my sister Marta
who read poetry to me
and our great-aunt Jessie
who read it to her

Tyger Tyger, burning bright,
In the forests of the night;
What immortal hand or eye,
Could frame thy fearful symmetry?

In what distant deeps or skies.
Burnt the fire of thine eyes?
On what wings dare he aspire?
What the hand, dare seize the fire?

And what shoulder, & what art,
Could twist the sinews of thy heart?
And when thy heart began to beat,
What dread hand? & what dread feet?

What the hammer? what the chain,

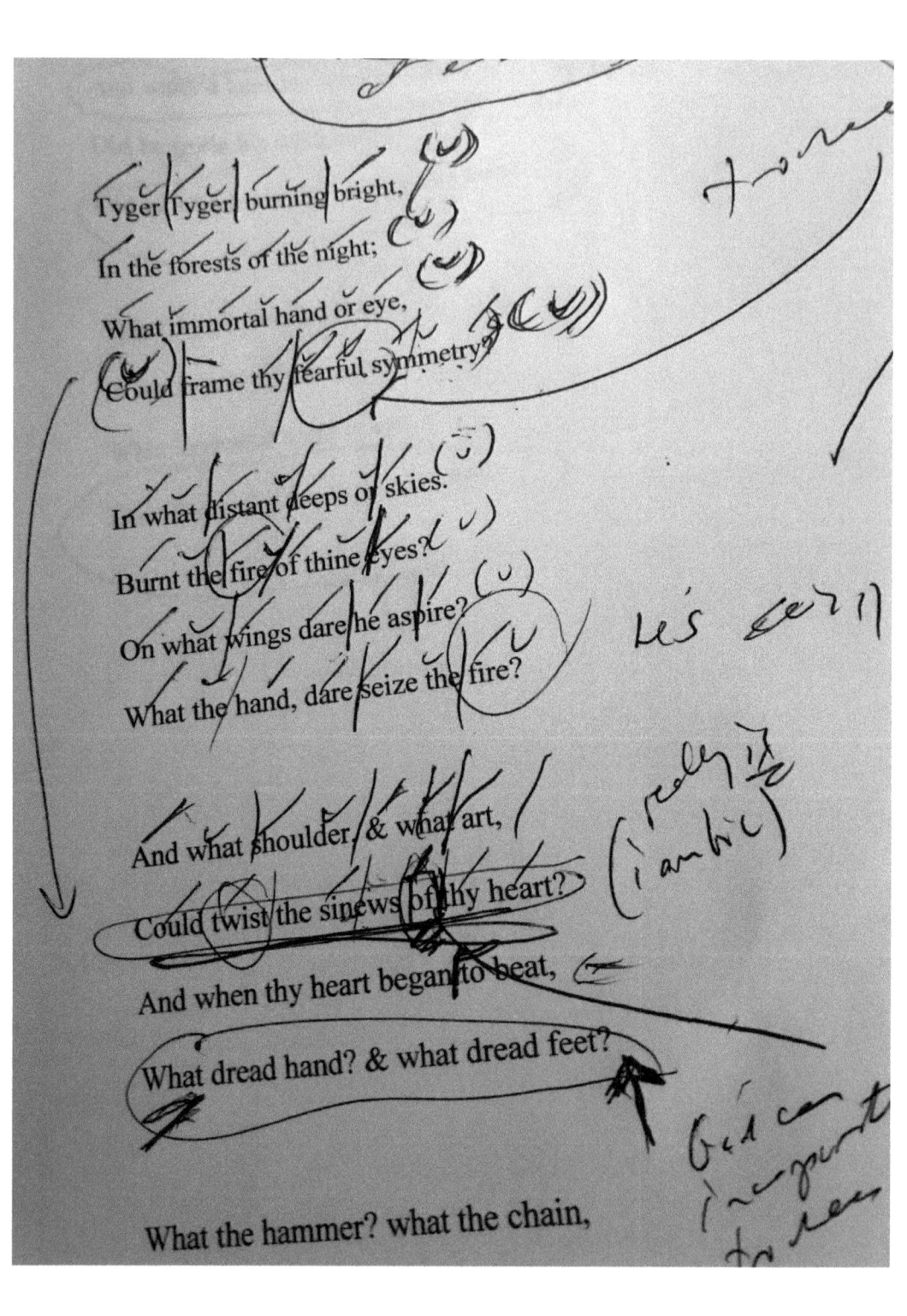

Some Related Books by Annie Finch

Prose

A Poet's Craft: A Comprehensive Guide to Making and Sharing Your Poetry
A Poet's Ear: A Handbook of Meter and Form
The Body of Poetry: Essays on Women, Form, and the Poetic Self
The Ghost of Meter: Culture and Prosody in American Free Verse

Poetry

Calendars: Poems by Annie Finch and Readers Guide with Scansions
Earth Days: Poems, Chants, and Spells in Five Directions
Spells: New and Selected Poems
Among the Goddesses: An Epic Libretto in Seven Dreams Eve

Anthologies

Measure for Measure: An Anthology of Poetic Meters Villanelles
An Exaltation of Forms: Contemporary Poets Celebrate the Diversity of Their Art
After New Formalism: Poets on Form, Narrative, and Tradition
A Formal Feeling Comes: Poems in Form by Contemporary Women

Please note: For copyright reasons as well as pedagogical reasons, the poems in this book are mostly classic poems in the public domain. If you seek contemporary poems in meter, check out the books above, especially *Measure for Measure, Villanelles,* and *A Formal Feeling Comes.*

CONTENTS

Foreword: How is This Book Different? ix

Introduction: Meter, Magic, and Scansion xiii

RESOURCES FOR REFERENCE xvii

Scansion Tools: A Quick Guide xvii

List of Metrical Feet xviii

Definitions of Key Terms xix

Guiding Principles of Scansion xxi

PART 1: ACCENTUALS 1

Chapter 1: Scanning Accentuals: The Foundation of Meter 3

PART 2: ACCENTUAL-SYLLABICS 17

Section 1 Introduction to The Three-Step Method 19

Section 2 Scansions 35

    Process for Doing the Scansions 35

    Poems to Scan 37

        Iambs 45

        Trochees 51

        Dactyls 61

        Amphibrachs 69

        Dipodics, Etc. 79

    Scanned Poems 83
        Iambs 94
        Trochees 101
        Dactyls 108
        Amphibrachs 118
        Dipodics, Etc. 129

Afterword: Beyond Scansion 133

Acknowledgments 137

Foreword

HOW IS THIS BOOK DIFFERENT?

How to Scan a Poem differs from other books on meter and scansion in two major ways:

1. *It is structured according to the principle of metrical diversity.* In this book, we recognize a "metrical compass" of different meters and honor them equally as different valid ways of writing, reading, and scanning metrical verse.

2. *It is informed by the principle of the metrical code.* Scansion in this book is not a mechanical exercise but instead an invitation to explore the deepest interactions between meter and meaning — and hence between form and energy, consciousness and spirit.

METRICAL DIVERSITY

Discussions of scansion these days are rare as hens' teeth, even in books about poetry. When they do occur, most either focus on iambic meter alone, or they privilege iambic (especially iambic pentameter) over any other meter, as if this meter enjoys a natural superiority to anapests, dactyls, trochees, amphibrachs, and the rest.

Over thirty years ago, I learned that iambic naturalness is a fantasy. I now understand that it is a sad and dangerous fantasy with serious implications, not only for poetry, but for the health and survival of our species on this earth. The full idea will be the subject of another book. Meanwhile, I will share a story.

Like many twentieth-century graduate programs in poetry writing, the one where I earned an MA in the mid 1980s—the University of Houston—was entirely devoted to free verse. The faculty published only free verse. The students—except for me, who had learned meter as an undergraduate but kept that a secret and had sneaked into the program with a free-verse writing sample—only wrote free verse. For some reason, though, the program required that every poet take a class in Versification.

I remember our teacher, Cynthia MacDonald, walking into class the first day with the words, "well, I know none of us wants to be here, but we may as well make the best of it." Very few of Cynthia's assignments involved meter—instead we counted syllables and wrote syllabics and haiku, or free-verse sestinas. The only conversation on meter I can recall is when she announced in chalky letters on the blackboard, "English falls naturally into iambics."

I stared, wondering when she would realize her mistake and erase it. But she didn't notice; nor did anyone else seem to. It would be decades before I grew the courage to speak up about meter. I simply sat there and let the truth sink in: my teacher was unable to recognize that she had just written on the board, in a sentence that fell naturally into perfect dactylic meter with a trochee in the last foot, an outright, self-contradicting lie.

That moment was the birth of my lifetime's passion for teaching meter—and especially for teaching what I have come to call "metrical diversity."

A few years later, during my Ph.D studies at Stanford, I made it a point to connect with some of the world's top prosodists and to settle the question of the iamb's assumed 'naturalness' in English once and for all. What I learned was that iambic meter enjoys zero linguistic advantage over other meters in English. Its privileges are inherited: cultural, political, and literary. All meters are potentially equally "natural."

That's why, in this book, we take a radically different approach from the mainstream. We will scan poems from the whole "compass" of five basic meters equally. This is not because equal numbers of poems currently exist in all these meters; iambic remains the most common of meters by far. It is because every meter's voice has something essential to share with us. As with biological diversity and cultural diversity, we ignore metrical diversity at our own peril.

Metrical diversity matters because, first of all, it offers a true and accurate picture of meter in the English language. Necessary poems have been written in the five basic meters covered in this book: anapestic, iambic, trochaic, dactylic, and amphibrachic—and in others as well. So, to ignore the noniambic meters and focus only on iambics is intellectually and aesthetically irresponsible.

Metrical diversity also matters on an energetic level. During my lifelong poetic journey, I have come to believe that our healing and survival—individually and as a planet – requires metrical diversity. Poetry's primal magic power arises from the fact that each meter has its own rhythmic pattern that shapes the energy of those who write it, read it, speak it, hear it, think it, dance it. English lags far behind some other languages in the range and variety of our magic metrical vocabulary, but the five meters that form the basis of this book are a start towards reclaiming our own metrical diversity.

THE METRICAL CODE

Not long after Cynthia's Versification class, with its glaring lesson in the hegemony of iambic meter, a teacher in my poetry workshop handed out copies of Emily Dickinson's "After great pain, a formal feeling comes." As I stared idly down at the afternoon light play across the familiar stanzas, suddenly I understood Dickinson's famous first line—an iambic pentameter—on a whole new level. I felt her words referring to their own meter, to the "formal feeling" of iambic pentameter that makes "the nerves sit ceremonious, like tombs." Having struggled with my own doubts over slipping into that familiar meter, I felt how the iambic meter carried some of the same burden for her as it did for me—and some of the same legacy of meaning.

That revelation began the gestation of my idea of the metrical code. In *The Ghost of Meter* (1993), based on my Stanford dissertation, I developed the idea through scansion of the work of Dickinson, Whitman, Eliot, Lorde, and other poets. By analyzing the meanings of lines in different meters, I traced how metrical patterns such as iambic and dactylic meters can carry unconscious cultural and historical messages Since then, in part through my own spiritual journey as a practicing witch, I have come to understand that meter's meanings are evident in metrical poetry as well as in free verse, and that they are spiritual and psychological as well as cultural.

All these meanings may be found weaving throughout the scansions in this book, for those interested to hear them. The correspondences I teach my students—those I have been developing over decades of ritual and poetic work with the five basic meters— are: anapests/will, iambs/mind, trochees/body, dactyls/heart, and amphibrachs/spirit. Many have found these correspondences useful; you may prefer others. The main priority is to make space for metrical diversity itself. It is through allowing room for all aspects of ourselves that we will heal and grow, both as individuals who write, read, and love poetry, and as a society coming back into touch with the necessary powers of its own poetic soul.

ABOUT THE POEMS IN THIS BOOK

The current hegemony of iambic meter in the English language dates from the time of the Renaissance, when it corresponded with the rise of imperialism, patriarchy, and nationalism on a global scale. When the Modernist poets of the early twentieth century finally "broke the [iambic] pentameter," to quote Ezra Pound, other meters did not arise to fill the vacuum as they had expected. Instead, we have experienced a century dominated by free verse, while those few poets who write in meter still cleave almost exclusively to iambic.

Due to my deep experience of the importance of metrical diversity, my own poetry is a conscious, enthusiastic exception to this rule. And I'm proud to cite increasing numbers of my own students, including Autumn Newman, Patricia Smith, Anna Lena Phillips Bell, Tamam Khan, Joanne Godley, Richelle Slota, and Joshua Davis, as further exceptions. Still, while editing *Measure for Measure: An Anthology of Poetic Meters (2010)*, in order not to include too many of my own poems I was forced to dig deep into decades of my files of poems in meter, search long and hard in out-of-print books, be responsible for reprint permissions, and cajole numerous colleagues and students to give writing in certain meters a try.

This book is not another wide-as-possible anthology. It is meant to complement *Measure for Measure* with a more intimate selection of metrical poems, in keeping with the intimate nature of scansion itself. Some of the scanned poems are my own; others are poems in the public domain that I have loved for years; and some are poems I admire by friends. All are poems whose meters sprang to mind of their own accord—poems whose meters are already etched into me. They were chosen because the thought of scanning them gave me joy—because I believe that scanning them can lead us to some of the widest and deepest places scansion can go.

Are you ready? Let's go there together.

Annie Finch
Brooklyn, NY
July 17, 2023

Introduction

METER, MAGIC, AND SCANSION

WHY SCAN?

Why scan a poem—either your own or someone else's? Because scansion is the best method—essentially, the only method— to really understand how the meter of a particular poem works its magic. If you are starting out writing in meter, scansion is essential for you to tell one foot from another, to recognize variations in the meter, and to build up your own rhythmic vocabulary so that your poems will express the mood and tone you want. And even after you are deeply familiar with meter, you will still need the tools of scansion to work out what is happening in particularly subtle or amazing passages of poetry, and to move forward through rhythmically challenging moments in your own poems.

Scanning is the most misunderstood aspect of poetry. Scansion is considered dry and dull and academic—and yet it is by far the most juicy, sensual, physically pulsating approach to poetry. Scansion is treated as analytical, apart from the creative process—and yet, for a poet, scansion allows the draft of a poem to actually communicate with itself, opening pathways to radical creative discoveries. Scansion is considered a way of thinking—and yet it is a way of hearing, a way of feeling, a way of listening, a way of dancing. Truly, scansion is a way of living. If meter is the stage on which the deepest change can happen in a poem, scansion adds the dimension of magical awareness that invites meaning to grow from change: expectation, pattern, and release.

Until the advent of free verse about a hundred years ago, poetic rhythm was so familiar in our bodies that scansion may not have been necessary. But —as I've learned over thousands of hours teaching meter—it's now a central tool for those of us who are serious about reclaiming the power of rhythmic language in our current world. In fact, scansion can be a first step to navigating our way back into the body familiarity that guides much of the wisdom of oral-based, earth-centered societies. Scansion matters.

What is scansion, exactly? Scansion is nothing more nor less than a deep, attentive listening to a poem's meter, the marking of its music. The mystery of pattern, the grounded presence of repetition, the joy of expectation, the gift of expectation satisfied—these are the sublime, indescribable gifts of meter. And scansion is the best way we have to experience them. Deep Scansion—exploring how scansion interacts with other levels of a poem—is the most powerful overlooked secret to reading, writing, loving, absorbing, and being transformed by the magic of poetry. I never get bored with the mysterious and ever-surprising experience of scanning a great poem.

Meter and other kinds of predictable, physically patterned repetition have been the distinguishing feature of poetry across cultures for many millenia—since long before the invention of writing. And it is from this era that the magical legacy of poetry begins. In fact, the words "meter" and "magic" both spring from the same proto-Indo-European root, *meh, meaning "power." During an era when meter helped poets to memorize the epics, legends, and healing and spiritual inheritance of their people, which otherwise would have been lost entirely, it is no wonder meter was regarded as magic and poets as direct channels to divine power. We know this to have been true in cultures around the globe, from the history in Homeric and Anglo-Saxon epics to the Aruyvedic hymns carrying precious medical knowledge in Sanskrit meter, to Native American creation tales, to the Yoruba sacred poetry where each divinity spoke in its own distinctive meter.

Because the innermost magical reality of a poem is a matter of rhythm--the unfolding of movement through time—to scan a poem is to navigate the fulcrum of its innermost reality. Scansion is how we translate the wordless, eloquent language of meter into our awareness, and deep scansion is the best way to go deeply into a poem for the first, or the hundredth, time.

In the same way that we experience the most sublime romantic and spiritual emotions as physical sensations in our bodies, a poem expresses its own most sublime truths in the physical sensations of the lengths, weights, and rhythms of its syllables. And it is only through scansion that we can truly experience these sensations in the same way the poet has done.

In this workbook, we will be learning scansion as a technique on the page. But scansion does not always have to happen on the page. Once you have learned the simple, mighty skills conveyed here, you will have all you need to bring scansion off the page and into your body, your ear, your breath, your heartbeat. With just a bit of practice, scansion will become part of your physical reality, and after that—although you may still enjoy scanning especially subtle or tricky poems using the written methods in this book—you will also be able to scan by nodding your head, tapping your fingers, dancing, or even just listening deeply.

When you scan in this physical way, you will be reclaiming one of the most ancient human birthrights on this planet—one still enjoyed by a good part of humanity, but lost to most of us who inhabit the W.E.I.R.D. (Western Educated Industrial Rich Democracies, to use the term coined by anthropologist Joseph Henrich). You will have freed yourself from the dominance of the mind and entered the beautiful flow-state in which will, mind, body, heart, and spirit are all equally powerful, equally important.

The tools of scansion you will learn in this book invite you to enter the poet's own voice, mind, and inner ear in the most intimate of ways, marking the time of the poem in their mind and weighing the counterpointing interplay of forces, between the template/pattern of the meter and the exact ways that a poet has inhabited and altered the shape of the meter to embody the poet's own bodily/emotional/spiritual reality in the unique moment.

RESOURCES FOR REFERENCE

SCANSION TOOLS: A QUICK GUIDE

(you'll find more detail about these tools on p. xx and throughout the book)

/ WAND   (stressed syllable, also sometimes called accent, stress, or ictus, and sometimes macron (which actually means 'long syllable')

u CUP   (unstressed syllable, also sometimes called unstress, nonictus, or breve (which actually means 'short syllable')

| EDGE   (foot-boundary, sometimes called footbreak)

\ HALF- WAND (secondary accent, sometimes called reversed accent, half-stress, or half-accent)

(u) GHOST CUP (missing *or extra* unstressed syllables, at beginning or end of a line)

REST (*very rare!* missing unstressed syllable within line)

|| CAESURA (midline pause—*very rare!* Used in scansion when a pause is an established, predictable part of the metrical pattern of each line, as in Anglo-Saxon prosody or Poe's "The Raven." Also, sometimes used to demonstrate the phrasal structures of poetic lines; but then, it marks the *rhythm* of words in individual lines, not their *meter* (relation to a predictable metrical pattern).

LIST OF METRICAL FEET

/u	trochee
u/	iamb
//	spondee
uu	pyrrhic
/uu	dactyl
uu/	anapest
u/u	amphibrach
/u/	cretic (also called amphimacer)
u//	bacchius
//u	antibacchius
///	molossos
uuu	tribrach
/uuu	first paeon
u/uu	second paeon
uu/u	third paeon
uuu/	fourth paeon
//uu	major ionic
uu//	minor ionic
u//u	antispast
u/u/	diamb
u///	first epitrite
/u//	second epitrite
//u/	third epitrite
///u	fourth epitrite
/uu/	choriamb
uuuu	tetrabrach (also called proceleus or maticus)
////	dispondee
/uuuu	Hardy (invented by Annie Finch and Autumn Newman while scanning for this book)

THREE BASIC TYPES OF FEET

Falling feet fall from stronger to weaker syllables (wands to cups). Examples: dactyl, trochee.

Rising feet rise from weaker to stronger syllables (cups to wands). Examples: anapest, iamb.

Rocking feet are the same at both ends and change in the middle. Example: cretic, amphibrach.

Most feet that are often used fit into one of these categories.

DEFINITIONS OF KEY TERMS

Rhythm: The sound-patterns created by the interplay of accented and unaccented syllables in spoken language, prose, or metrical or nonmetrical poetry. Like waves in the ocean, rhythm can sometimes sound quite regular, but it is never regular enough to be fully predictable.

Meter: Predictable repetition of patterns of syllables based on perceptible physical differences. While meter can theoretically be based on any language element for experimental purposes (e.g. Marianne Moore's syllabic meter), most meter arises organically from the repetition of characteristics that are meaningful within its language

Foot: A single instance of a repeating pattern created by perceptible physical differences among syllables.

Metrical Contract: An unspoken understanding between poet and listener/reader that the metrical pattern established in first few lines of a poem will continue throughout the poem, unless there's a worthy aesthetic/poetic reason for it to be broken.

Base Meter: A metrical pattern that is predictable and usually perceptible usually consisting of one type of metrical foot that is repeated a certain number of times per line(e.g. accentual trimeter, dactylic hexameter, anapestic dimeter, alternating iambic tetrameter and trimeter(a.k.a.ballad meter), trochaic octometer with a medial caesura, etc).

Cadence: A metrical pattern created by combining at least two metrical feet in a certain order. While the poetry of some languages, such as Hindi, uses numerous cadences. English currently has only a few in common use, most familiarly the Hendecasyllabic (trochee-dactyl-trochee-trochee-trochee) and two lines used in the Sapphic stanza, the Sapphic line (trochee-trochee-dactyl-trochee-trochee) and the Adonic (dactyl-trochee).

En-rhythming: The process of accustoming one's ear and body to the sound of a particular rhythm in preparation for writing, reading, or scanning that meter. This can be done through reading aloud poems composed in that meter or through drumming, tapping, or moving to the rhythm.

Metrical Trust: A reader/listener's level of openness to the physical experience of a metrical poem, as earned/established by the metrical contract.

Metrical Variation: (also called substitution): an altering in the expected metrical foot, for aesthetic and/or expressive purposes.

Metrical Suspense: A disturbance in the reader/listener's level of metrical trust, created by one or more challenging metrical variations that seem to approach the breaking of the metrical contract but don't actually break it [e.g. the first line of Shakespeare's Sonnet 116].

Metrical Resolution: Reaffirming of the metrical contract through a regular line of meter, after a period of metrical suspense [e.g. the second line of Shakespeare's Sonnet 116].

Foot-Building: The way a poem prepares the listener/reader to experience certain kinds of variations in feet, especially feet that are not part of the expected metrical pattern, by building up to them (e.g. a series of two or three spondees in preceding lines may build up to a mid-line trochee in an iambic poem)

Metrical Climax: the point at which a metrical training that has been building intersects with the verbal meaning and emotional tones of a poem to create a crucial shift or transformation in the poem.

Performative Accent: (or performative stress). How people emphasize certain syllables when we speak a phrase, to express our emotions or thoughts. Because the pressure of meter can encourage or even force someone to emphasize various syllables, meter can profoundly affect performative stress, and therefore meaning.

Deep Scansion: Scanning the meter of a poem in close relationship to the poem's meaning at every point, and vica versa; checking in with the effect of each scansion choice on the poem's meaning as you go, and allowing that knowledge to guide the subsequent scansion choices in the poem.

GOALS AND GUIDING PRINCIPLES OF SCANSION

Three Goals of Scansion

1. To show how the poet has followed the poem's base meter.

2. To show if and how the poet has varied the base meter.

3. To make any scansion choices that may be needed in light of the deepest possible understanding of the poem's meanings.

Five Guiding Principles of Scansion

In order of importance. When making a tricky scansion decision, move in this order, and keep all the principles in mind as far as possible. Ideally, most scansion choices will adhere to all of these principles.

1. **Principle of Line-Length.** A scansion needs above all to respect the number of feet per line of the base meter, as established in the metrical contract.

2. **Principle of Simplicity**. After Principle1 is met, the best scansion is the simplest. The simplest scansion is the scansion that has the lowest number of variations from the base meter. For example,

3. **Principle of Direction.** After Principles1 and 2 are met, the best scansion is the one that follows the direction of the base meter: whether the meter is basically falling (trochees, dactyls, and other feet that begin with a wand), rising (anapests, iambs, other feet that end with a wand) or rocking (amphibrachs, cretics, and other feet that are the same at beginning and end but change in the middle). For example, here's a line by Thomas Hardy: "even to the original air-blue gown." At first glance, it may seem natural to scan the first three syllables as an anapest. But the line occurs in "The Voice," a poem with a base meter of dactylic tetrameter—a falling rhythm. Not only would that anapest contradict the poem's overall falling direction; it would also force the two subsequent feet to be anapests also, and the final foot to be an iamb-- all rising feet instead of falling. Instead, we scan the opening syllables as a Hardy (/ uuuu). Yes, this scansion actually required the invention of a new foot --the first foot I have ever invented, which I think Hardy, a poet so dedicated to formal diversity that he used the vast majority of his poetic forms only once, might have appreciated. The use of the Hardy leads to a better scansion since it enables the remainder of the line

to be scanned in falling meter (dactyl-trochee-tailless dactyl), respecting the way the line moves with the poem's overall falling rhythm. Although the anapestic rhythm is still felt in the words as a fascinating countercurrent, it is not marked in the scansion.

4. **Principle of Metrical Context.** An unusual metrical variation will often make more sense within the metrical context of the poem—and sometimes within the poet's work as a whole. See "Foot-Building" in the defintiions above.

5. **Principle of Meaning**. A good scansion, especially one that involves a tricky or difficult scansion choice, ideally illuminates and deepens the meaning of a poem, both in its own moment and in the poem as a whole.

A FEW NICKNAMES

Please skip this section if you are new to scansion—it's just meant for fun after you already know everything else in this book! These are not actual metrical feet, since they gain their metrical identities only as *variations* of feet. Still, when scanning or discussing scansions, these terms (invented by Annie and Autumn during the long process of doublechecking the Scansions section) may come in handy as shorthand nicknames:

Half-trochee: A trochee with a half-wand replacing a cup

Half-iamb: an iamb with a half-wand replacing a cup

Half-cretic: a dactyl or anapest with a half-wand replacing the final cup (in a dactyl) or the first cup (in an anapest)

Ghost trochee: a trochaic foot in which a ghost cup replaces the cup [found at the end of a line—if in mid-line, the ghost cup would become a rest]

Ghost dactyl: a dactylic foot in which a ghost cup replaces the final cup [found at the end of a line—if in mid-line, the ghost cup would become a rest]

Double ghost dactyl: a dactylic foot in which ghost cups replace both cups [found at the end of a line—if in mid-line, the ghost cups would become a rest]

Resty iamb—iamb with a rest replacing the cup

Resty trochee—trochee with a rest replacing the cup

Light trochee—one of the lighter alternating trochees in dipodic trochaic meter

Heavy trochee—one of the heavier alternating trochees in dipodic trochaic meter

Light iamb—one of the lighter alternating iambs in dipodic iambic meter

Heavy iamb—one of the heavier alternating iambs in dipodic iambic meter

PART 1

ACCENTUALS

Chapter 1

SCANNING ACCENTUALS: THE FOUNDATION OF METER

One of the magical aspects of meter is that, in every language, poetic meter is based on the *working* aspects of the language: those aspects that carry meaning. For example, tone (syllable pitch) carries meaning in the Chinese language, so Chinese poetic meter involves contrasting tones. In English, however tone does not carry meaning. So English meter does not involve tone. Instead, the core element of English-language meter is a very hard working aspect of the English language: accent.

What is accent? You clearly already know the answer because, as someone who can read English, you recognize and use accent in every English word of more than one syllable. The word "encounter," for example, has three syllables: en-count-er. One of these syllables has an accent, meaning that it is more heavily stressed, or emphasized, than the other two. Which syllable do you feel this is? If you're not sure, you can look in the dictionary, which will show an accent mark over –you've probably already guessed it—the second syllable.

Recognizing and distinguishing accent is the first step in learning to scan English-language poetry. It's not so much a matter of perceiving accent. Accent is so basic to English that if we couldn't recognize accent, we not be able to use the English language at all. Many of us don't realize the inherent skill we already have in perceiving accent. If you are eating a dessert in a desert, how do you avoid a mouthful of sand? What if you want to go into an old-fashioned music studio and record a record? Anyone who uses the English language perceives accent untold numbers of times every day. So our goal is learning to reliably trust our perceptions of accent and become aware of them.

To go a little deeper into the question of what accent is, think about how you would describe the difference between "count" and the other two syllables of "encounter." Many of us would say that "count" is louder. But if you try to say the word while pronouncing all three syllables equally loudly, you will probably notice that you can still, somehow, tell that "count" has a special emphasis. How did you do this, when they are equally loud? Linguists tell us that accent is a more complex phenomenon than volume alone. Actually, accent has three different components: loudness, length, and pitch. Depending on the syllable and context, any one two, or three of these factors can play its part in our perception of accent. An accented syllable is louder, longer, and/or higher pitched than the syllables around it. A good way to explore how this works for you will be to read this list of heteronyms aloud, noticing which aspects of each syllable your meter antenna picks up.

HETERONYMS: GETTING IN TOUCH WITH YOUR EAR FOR ACCENT

Read these pairs of words that look the same but have different meanings aloud:

    console (verb), console (noun)
    entrance (noun), entrance (verb)
    combine (verb), combine (noun)
    protest (noun), protest (verb)
    exploit (verb), exploit (noun)
    minute (adjective), minute (noun)
    confines (verb), confines (noun)
    increase (noun), increase (noun)
    contract (verb), contract (noun),
    decrease (noun), decrease (verb)
    conflict (noun), conflict (verb)
    convict (verb), convict (noun)
    conduct (noun), conduct (verb)

If, during the course of this book, you ever find yourself feeling that you can't distinguish accented from unaccented syllables, just go back to this section and read this list until you get your confidence back. If you can get by with speaking English to others every day, then there is absolutely nothing wrong with your perceptions of accent. For most of us, any feeling of confusion about accent arises not from lack of knowledge but from the opposite problem: over thinking, putting our minds where our bodies should be. If there is one lesson I hope you will learn from this book, it is to relax, to trust your perceptions and your body, and above all to enjoy. When you are really stuck figuring out which syllable is the stressed one, here are two tricks that my students and I have found very helpful over the years:

TWO TRICKS FOR HEARING ACCENT

1. **Reverse Exaggeration Method**: Say you are trying to figure out which syllable of the word "because" should be accented. Speak the word aloud, exaggerating the difference between the syllables. To get enough aural space for the contrast, you will need to whisper the first syllable very softly and then shout the second syllable as loudly as you can depending on where you are: beCAUSE!. Then do the same thing in reverse (BEcause!) Which sounds more natural?

2. **Shout-across-the-Room Method**: Imagine you're shouting the word or phrase to a friend who's across a large room. To make it even more effective, embed the word in a natural sentence: "I love you because you're awesome!" Which syllable of the word are you stressing?

One area in which we tend to very confident about distinguishing accent is when it comes to the pronunciation of our own names. Let's try a simple exercise.

NAME SCANNING EXERCISE

1. WRITE YOUR NAME. (use any version of your first, middle, and/or last name that you like—the longer the better. It's fine to make up extra names for yourself and add those in as well—why not use this moment to treat yourself to your magical dream name at last?

2. SAY your name aloud a few times until you're sure, and then write it again and, using a pencil, put a WAND (accent mark) over the most strongly accented syllables.

3. Now copy it a final time in pencil, including the wands, and put a CUP (lower-case u) over all the remaining syllables.

4. While looking at #3, ask someone else to say your name aloud to you., or say it to yourself aloud. Do the wands and cups match up with the stronger and weaker syllables you are speaking? If necessary, erase and fix them. If you get confused, take a break and come back to it later.

YOUR METER ANTENNA

*The most important single rule of scansion is to listen more than you think: keep your mind in its place, and always trust your meter antenna. Where is your meter antenna? When you read a poem aloud, it may feel as if your antenna is connected to your physical ears, but it doesn't have to be. Your meter antenna can also be your inner ear, a kind of voice you hear in your mind. Or it can be the feeling in your mouth when you whisper or say the words. Or it might be a response you feel somewhere else in your body, like a leap in your heart. Where's **your** meter antenna?*

Now that you have gotten in touch with your meter antenna and the other ways you recognize meter, it's time to put these skills into practice with a poem. We will start with a poem composed in accentual meter. I say "composed," rather than "written," because many poems are never meant to be written down at all—especially accentual poems, which are the closest to the ancient oral-based poetic traditions of our language. Meter allowed poets to keep safe, share, and pass along untold numbers of epics and legends, Untold amounts of knowledge, centuries of secrets and prayers, in every part of the world long before the invention of writing. Homer's *Iliad* and *Odyssey*, epic poems of the Phillipines, African praise-songs, the *Kalevala* of Finland, Aruyvedic hymns full of medical lore in India, and the Anglo-Saxon *Beowulf* all reveal techniques of metered composition, a technology by which poets create, remember, and pass down to future generations poems that may take hours, days, or even weeks to recite.

In the English language, as is appropriate to a language in which accent plays a central role, the meters of oral tradition are based on patterns of accent. *Beowulf* and other early English-language poems are written in accentual meter, which means there are the same number of accented syllables in every line. This is a common approach to meter for poems meant to be read aloud or performed, including nursery rhymes and contemporary rap music.

SCANNING ACCENTUALS

To scan an accentual poem, you need just one tool, the first tool on your Scansion Tools list: the **wand.**

Here's a little accentual poem, to give you the idea. Just mark a wand over each strong accent. Then count up the wands on each line, and you should find there are the same number in each line.

>Rain, rain, go away,
>
>Come again some other day,
>
>Little Poet wants to play.

To complete a scansion, we label the poem with the name of its meter. In the case of an accentual poem, the meter's name is the word Accentual, followed by a word indicating the number of accents per line: monometer, dimeter, trimeter, tetrameter, pentameter, hexameter, heptameter, octometer. So, after putting a wand over each accented syllable in the poem above, you would label it Accentual Tetrameter.

What would be the name of the meter of this poem? If you're not sure, follow the steps in "How to Scan an Accentual Poem," below:

>The eensie weensie spider
>
>Went up the water spout
>
>Down came the rain
>
>And washed the spider out.
>
>Out came the sun
>
>And dried up all the rain
>
>And the eensie weensie spider
>
>Went up the spout again

Here's another example, from a children's game:

Little Sally Walker

Walking down the street.

She didn't know what to do

So she stopped in front of me.

She said, "Hey girl, do your thing,

Do your thing and switch!

Hey girl do your thing

Do your thing and switch!"

When scanning an accentual poem, here are the steps to follow:

HOW TO SCAN AN ACCENTUAL POEM

1. #Speakitthrice (recommended) It's a good idea to start any scansion by reading the poem, or at least the beginning if it's a very long poem, aloud at least once. My recommendation is always to read it three times, which is why you'll see the hashtag #speakitthrice on my Twitter feed and elsewhere. This will get the poem into your body and wake up your meter antenna, and it will alert you to patterns. .

2. The next step is to doublespace the poem so you will have room for the scansion marks. When scanning on your own, you can use cut-and-paste or write it out with plenty of room. Here, it will be done for you.

3. The next step is to go through the poem, reading aloud, and put a **wand** on the syllables that feel the strongest/most stressed. Put your wand right above the syllable and in the exact center of it. If you are scanning by hand, use a pencil in case you need to erase a mistake. If you are scanning onscreen, type the symbol on the in-between line and use the keys to move it to the exact location you need. At this point, just use your ear/antenna to guide you; don't overthink it. You will have time to doublecheck later.

4. Scan one line at a time, and look for patterns as you go. If you have 4 wands in one line, or 3, then open yourself to find for the same number of wands in the following line. But be careful! Sometimes our Mind will jump right in and say," Oh great, we're looking for 4 accents in every line? I can do that!" and start putting wands in before your meter antenna even has a chance to absorb the line. If that happens, stop your mind immediately. You might tell it something like, "I know you're trying to help, but you're not helping. Stop that right now. My meter antenna's got this. As soon as it's time for your help, I will be sure to ask you. Thanks!"

5. As you listen for wands, aim for an attitude of open curiosity. Try feeling that you are dancing **with** the meter—not submitting to it or controlling it, but enjoying free, equal interaction.. You may want to use your body, tap your foot, get up and move as you feel into the rhythm and which syllables it lands on. Sometimes you will need to try it several ways before it truly clicks into place. When it does click into place, you'll know.

6. If you get confused because it seems like everything should get an accent, add more water in the stream bed. This is my favorite metaphor for how meter works. Since I wrote it in my book *A Poet's Craft*, it has been useful to many, many poets. Think of a line of poetry as the bed of a rocky stream or arroyo, lined with stones of many different sizes, large, medium, and small. In the spring when there's a lot of water in the stream, only the biggest rocks will show above the water, and the others will be hidden. But in late summer when the stream is dry, you might see every single rock, even the smallest ones. Imagine that in your stream of poetry, you control the water level. If you are noticing accents all over the place, imagine pouring water into your stream so that only the biggest rocks, the strongest accents—the loudest, longest, highest-pitched accents—are visible above the water. These are where you will put your wands. On the other hand, if you are having trouble hearing any accents at all, your stream has too much water in it. Imagine draining some of the water out so the strongest accents will rise above the others, like big rocks reaching out of the water that hides the others. The Accent Hierarchy Guide below can help you decide which rocks are the biggest—though the **sound** always takes precedence!

7. When you have marked each line, go back and read the poem aloud and check if the wands seem to match the reality of how you speak it. A great way to do this is to give your scanned copy to someone else. Then you read the poem aloud in

a natural voice, and have them check to see if you are actually stressing the same syllables where you have put your wands. Then switch places.

8. As a final step, count the number of accents you marked in each line of the poem. Does every line have the same number of accents? If not, do you see a regular pattern in the difference (such as, 4 accents, 3 accents, 4 accents, 3 accents in each 4-line stanza)? If you see a regular pattern, your scansion is probably a solid one. If you don't find a regular pattern, look at each line that doesn't fit. Is there another way you could say the line—maybe by adding water or releasing water from the streambed—that would make it fit with the pattern of the other lines? Remember, the point is not to force anything. All we are doing is observing and asking questions. If the poem is intended to be in meter, and was written by a poet who knows what they are doing, most of the time you will find the way to pronounce the line that fits the meter, and you can adjust your scansion accordingly—and often-- because meter, of course, affects how you pronounce and understand the line--you will have discovered something amazing and true about the meaning of the line in the process.

9. What if none of that works, and this line really is different? There are a few possibilities. A. The poem is not really in meter at all—it just looks like it. B. The poem is in meter, but there is a typo or other error, or the poet has simply disregarded the "metrical contract" (the unspoken agreement between a metrical poet and a reader that the basic outlines of the meter will be observed throughout the poem). C. Maybe the poem is so artful that the "mistake" enhances it on a deeper level. To investigate this possibility, meditate on the meaning of the line that's different. How does the change in meter change the line's meaning? Is there a reason that it might make sense for the line to have a different emphasis than the rest of the poem? Your feeling can be the guide to whether the metrical variation makes the poem more meaningful.

When you were scanning "Little Sally Walker," how did it go? Probably the first line was easy: 3 stresses. For the second line, did you put wands immediately over "walk and "street" ? But maybe you weren't so sure about "down"? If you drain just a tiny bit of water out of the streambed, it might feel quite natural to put one on "down," also, keeping a pattern of 3 wands in a line. This is not "cheating" or "forcing"—it's dancing with the meter, feeling your way towards a sense of the poem as a whole, opening yourself to the rhythmic pulse that knits it together like a heartbeat.

The next two lines are trickier. They could have either 3 or 4 beats, depending on whether you choose "She" at the beginning of line 3 and "So" at the beginning of line 4. Those choices would turn these lines into 4 beat lines. Thinking about step 9 of the Steps of Scansion above, it's interesting that in line 3 Sally "didn't know what to do"—just like the meter doesn't quite know what to do. But still…3 or 4 wands? In the spirit of curiosity and dancing with the meter, what would happen if you decided to hear it as 3 instead of 4? That would mean removing the wands from the first syllables of lines 3 and 4, and putting them on the second syllables of those lines instead.

Just try it out. Isn't it fun?

On a meaning level, the change takes the energy and attention off of "she" and puts it into the activity itself. And in fact, that is the way the song is traditionally sung on thousands of playgrounds—with strong stresses on "didn't" and "stopped." That these stresses have to be a little stronger to cover the extra syllables on "She" and "so" is what gives the lines their stronger, more compelling energy. Since the words "she said" in line 5 are extra words, spoken very quickly, they don't get accents. So the remainder of the lines should fit into the 3-beat pattern as well.

ACCENT HIERARCHY GUIDE

In a word of more than one syllable, the primary stress almost always takes precedence over any monosyllabic word in the line

With monosyllabic words, this is the usual order of stresses (most to last stress):

Nouns

Verbs

Adjectives

Adverbs

Pronouns

Prepositions

Conjunctions

Articles

METER AND THE LEVELS OF SPEECH ACCENT

There are three basic levels of speech accent:

Lexical Accent: This is the kind of accent that's marked in the dictionary on words of more than one syllable. The dictionary shows that the word "invisible" will always have the same accent pattern: u / u \. Nothing can contradict it; nobody can ever make it correct to pronounce this word with the accent on the third syllable, u u / u. However, since accent is always relative to other accents nearby, stronger accents next to the word "invisible" can overshadow one or sometimes even both of its stresses. And the momentum of meter further heightens the power of some accents to overshadow others. For example, if the word "invisible" appears in the line, "How bright invisible suns shine," we will clearly hear both accents. But if it appears in "We urge the invisible dragons to fly," the secondary accent on its fourth syllable will be overshadowed due to the meter. And if it appears in the line, "This is the forest invisible, the murmuring pines and the hemlocks" (apologies to Longfellow!), both accents will be almost entirely overshadowed. Meter can't change lexical stress, but it can affect the extent to which we hear it.

Phrasal Accent: This kind of accent results from sentence syntax, idiomatic phrases, and other demands of language for which speakers share a common understanding. Although these accent patterns don't appear in any dictionary, they work pretty much the same as lexical accent: they can't really be altered, only overshadowed. The accent hierarchy guide above shows the commonly accepted way of accenting parts of speech. With idioms, the momentum of tradition is even stronger. Think of an idiomatic phrase like "I told you so." Pronounced without stressing the second syllable, it would be unrecognizable to most people. So just as with lexical stress, scansions, like metrical poets, needs to work *with* phrasal accent patterns in order to do a credible and authentic job. That's not to say the accepted hierarchies might not be able to be bent sometimes—but any bending would need to be done in a creative spirit, with awareness and care.

Performative Accent: On this flexible, expressive level of accent, meter can truly do magical things. Performative accent is the way people emphasize certain syllables when we speak, to express our emotions or thoughts. The flexibility is especially clear with monosyllabic words. For example, when we say "I love you," we can choose to emphasize any of the 3 syllables with our tone of voice. The choice will change the meaning. And because the pressure of meter can encourage or even force someone to emphasize any of syllables, meter can affect performative stress, and therefore meaning. I can't think of any other way besides writing metrical poetry that we can actually get inside another person's vocal apparatus and make them use performative stress in a certain way. For example, here are three ways that meter could change the meaning of the phrase "I love you":

Trochaic:

Want to know why I'm so special?
I love you like no-one else does!

Amphibrachic:

I've finally learned something about this strange feeling:
I love you, there's no other way to describe it!

Anapestic:

In a world full of people, I only want you—
I love you, only you, and no other will do!

Here are some accentual poems to practice scanning. Later, you can check your scanned versions against the ones at the back of the book.

Anonymous

THIRTY DAYS HATH SEPTEMBER

Thirty days hath September

April, June and November

All the rest have thirty-one

Save February, and it alone,

Has twenty-eight we do confine

Till Leap Year gives it twenty nine.

Annie Finch

ANOTHER RELUCTANCE

Chestnuts fell in the charred season,

fell finally, finding room

in air to open their old cases

so they gleam out from the gold leaves

in the dust now, where they dropped down.

I go watch them, waiting for winter,

Their husks open and holding on.

Those rusted rims are rigid-hard

And cling clean to the clear brown.

But the fall sun sinks soon

And the day draws to its dark end,

And the feet give up the gray walk,

No longer lingering, light gone.

And I am here and do not go home.

Hollow gifts to cold children:

The chestnuts they hid in small caches

have gone hollow, their grain gone,

their gleam gone, and the children are home.

Edna St. Vincent Millay

RECUERDO

We were very tired, we were very merry—

We had gone back and forth all night on the ferry.

It was bare and bright, and smelled like a stable—

But we looked into a fire, we leaned across a table,

We lay on a hill-top underneath the moon;

And the whistles kept blowing, and the dawn came soon.

We were very tired, we were very merry—

We had gone back and forth all night on the ferry.

And you ate an apple, and I ate a pear,

From a dozen of each we had bought somewhere;

And the sky went wan, and the wind came cold,

And the sun rose dripping, a bucketful of gold.

We were very tired, we were very merry—

We had gone back and forth all night on the ferry.

We hailed, "Good morrow, mother!" to a shawl-covered head,

And bought a morning paper, which neither of us read;

And she wept, "God bless you!" for the apples and pears,

And we gave her all our money but our subway fares.

PART 2

ACCENTUAL-SYLLABICS

Section 1

INTRODUCTION TO THE THREE-STEP METHOD

Scansion is the process of recognizing and marking the meter we experience in a metrical poem. Poet Sidney Lanier invented a method of scansion that used musical notes to indicate exactly how long it took to pronounce different syllables. Some linguistically oriented prosodists mark every syllable with a number from 1 to 4 indicating the strength of its accent. Vladimir Nabokov developed a double row of scansion marks to show the tension meter creates between the expected pattern and actual stresses. While such idiosyncratic systems can highlight interesting aspects of meter, the most longstanding and widely-known system of scansion—the one we will learn in this book, which I call the Cup and Wand System—is widely considered to be the most flexible, accurate, and efficient way to scan poetry.

Based on marking softer and stronger syllables, and organizing the repeating patterns they make into "feet," the Cup-and-Wand System is simple and intuitive enough to be learned fairly easily. It is adaptable enough to mark the full range of metrical variations employed by poets, while also leaving room to express the unique perspective of the person doing the scanning. And the marks themselves have an elegance and rhythm that can make scanning with these symbols, especially with the three-step method, a deeply meditative process that brings us fully into the moment while leading us deep into the realm of a poem.

The particular approach to the Cup-and-Wand System we will learn here—The Three-Step Method of Scansion—was taught to me as an undergraduate at Yale by my Versification teacher, Penelope Laurans. She in turn based it on the work of her husband the poet Robert Fitzgerald, who taught it in his legendary Versification course at Harvard University for many years. We will be following Penny's Three-Step Method of Scansion throughout this book.

If you follow the three steps in the order given here until you know a particular meter inside out, and then move to scanning poems in the next meter, you will build a strong and accurate foundation for understanding, appreciating, and writing in a full range of meters. And eventually, after you are deeply familiar with a meter, you will probably be able to recognize the meter and encompass it rhythmically without needing to follow these steps every time—though you will always want to use the steps in this order for tricky scansion situations.

TOOLS

We will start with 2 lines, and the three most basic scansion tools:

Wand /

Cup u

Edge |

THE THREE-STEP METHOD

Step 1. Mark the accents with Wands.

Listen for where you hear the strong accents in each line (feel free to return to the Accentuals chapter for a refresher). Mark each strong accent with a wand over the middle of the syllable, just as you did for accentual poetry. Use a half-wand if a regular wand seems too strong for that syllable. It may help you to hear the accents if you exaggerate the rhythm of the poem: say a few lines aloud while SHOUTING the strongest accents and whispering the unstressed syllables. Remember, your ear, not your brain, is the ultimate authority; only mark the accents you would hear accented in natural speech! Tip: remember to put all the marks directly over the middles of their syllables to avoid confusion.

EXAMPLE: Step 1. Lines with only the accented syllables (Wands) marked

```
         /     /    /
We're learning how to scan

        /       /      /
With wands, and cups, and edges
```

EXERCISE:

Now mark the accents yourself, on these lines:

With ear and hand and eye

Until the pattern's clear

Step 2. Mark the remaining syllables with cups

The remaining syllables are unstressed, so mark them with cups.

EXAMPLE: Here are the lines with both wands and cups marked.

  u   / u / u /
We're learning how to scan

  u   / u / u / u
With wands, and cups, and edges

EXERCISE:

Copy the wands you added before to these other lines. Then fill in the cups.

With ear and hand and eye

Until the pattern's clear

Step 3. Look for repeating patterns of wands and cups. When you see a pattern repeat, separate it with the edge symbol (|).

These basic repeating patterns are called metrical feet. It's as if the feet are walking the poem along. Mark the boundaries between the metrical feet with your next scansion mark, the Edge. If the foot changes right in the middle of a word, go ahead and put the edge right down through the middle of the word if you are scanning by hand, or just above the middle of the word if you are using a keyboard. (Sometimes there may seem to be more than one way to divide the feet. If you have a choice, always choose the way that gives the same number of feet as the other lines in poem; for further guidance, see "Guiding Principles of Scansion" at the beginning of the book.)

EXAMPLE: Lines with all foot-boundaries marked. We see that the repeating pattern is this: cup-wand, u / Consulting the list of feet at the beginning of the book, we see this pattern is called the iamb. Notice there is one extra cup at the end of the second line. We will talk about that under "Finishing Touches."

u   / | u / | u /
We're learning how to scan

 u   / | u / | u / u
With wands, and cups, and edges

EXERCISE:

Copy the Wands and Cups you put before, and add the Edges to these other lines.

With ear and hand and eye

Until the pattern's clear

WHY THE ORDER OF THE THREE STEPS MATTERS

The genius of Penny's Three-Step Method of scansion is that it forces you to trust your body more than your mind. To mark the wands first, you must listen to each syllable with your ear or inner ear before you begin to think about the larger pattern at work. Therefore, the system forestalls the most common mistake people make when scanning: forgetting to listen in the body, instead letting the mind take over by deciding, "oh this is such-and-such a meter." The mind taking over leads to marking syllables mechanically, based on an abstract idea instead of tangible reality. The three-step method is a kind of insurance to make sure you stay honest, listen first, and don't let your mind run ahead of your ear. It is valuable to learn at the introductory level and also works well in tricky scansion situations. The three-step method will stand you in good stead throughout your life of scanning. Just remember to **follow the steps *in order***, especially when you are learning, and anytime you are unsure how to scan something.

FINISHING TOUCHES: GHOST CUPS

Your scansion is basically done. Sometimes, all you need to do at this point is to name it: figure out which foot is repeating (in this case, iambs) and how many per line (in this case, four), and put them together to find the meter's name (in this case, iambic tetrameter). But sometimes, once you know what the foot is, you will need to do some cleaning up to make sure that the scansion accurately recognizes/expresses/honors any variations in the line.

Poets don't always follow the pattern exactly—they use what's called "expressive variation" to create more moving and original poems. **Basically, a scansion has two jobs: 1. To show how the poet has followed the poem's base meter. 2. If needed, to show how the poet has varied the base meter.** In our little example, there is one variation from the meter: that extra cup.

In order to show how the poem varies the expected "base" meter of four iambs per line, we need to acknowledge the way the extra cup varies from the base meter. We do this by putting the Cup in parentheses. I call this a "Ghost Cup." A ghost cup is any cup at either the beginning or end of a line that is not part of the expected metrical pattern. Ghost cups can be either extra cups or missing cups—we mark them both the same way, with parentheses around them (if there are more than one in a row, they share one set of parentheses) For missing cups, the ghost cup marks go above the empty space to show that something is missing. For extra cups—such as we have here--we put the ghost cup mark just above the syllable as in regular scansion, with the parentheses showing they are extra. [One more thing, just so you know, while we are on the subject of ghost cups: ghost cups almost always appear at the beginnings or ends of lines. In the very rare cases where a ghost cup happens in the middle of a line, to avoid visual confusion we use a different symbol, the Rest, named after a rest in music. It looks like a hashtag: #   ]

So our final step now is to name the line, and to put parentheses around the ghost cup to show it is not part of the pattern. Note that we don't mark off a ghost cup with an edge, because a ghost cup does not make a new "foot" on its own (a foot needs to have at least one wand in order to qualify as a foot. Like other "rules" of scansion, this one is simply a matter of common physical sense: without a wand, our ears or inner ears will not hear/recognize it as a foot).

u   / | u   / | u   /
We're learning how to scan

 u   / | u   / | u   / (u)
With wands, and cups, and edges

Congratulations! You are scanning!

Now let's scan a slightly longer poem in another meter.

THE THREE-STEP METHOD, AGAIN

Step 1. Mark the accents with wands.

EXAMPLE: Step 1. Lines with only the accented syllables (wands) marked

/   /   /   /
In the season leaves should love,

/   /   /   /
since it gives them leave to move

/   /   /   /
through the wind, towards the ground

/   /   /   /
they were watching while they hung,

/   /   /   /
legend says there is a seam

/   /   /   /
stitching darkness like a name.

--from "Samhain" by Annie Finch

EXERCISE:

Now mark the accents yourself, on another passage from the same poem:

Now when dying grasses veil

earth from the sky in one last pale

wave, as autumn dies to bring

winter back, and then the spring,

we who die ourselves can peel

back another kind of veil

Step 2. Mark the remaining syllables with cups

EXAMPLE: Here is the opening of "Samhain" with both wands and cups marked.

/ u / u /   u   /
In the season leaves should love,

/   u / u / u /
since it gives them leave to move

/   u / u / u /
through the wind, towards the ground

/ u / u / u /
they were watching while they hung,

/ u / u / u /
legend says there is a seam

/   u / u / u /
stitching darkness like a name.

EXERCISE:

Copy the wands you added before to this other section of "Samhain." Then fill in the cups.

Now when dying grasses veil

earth from the sky in one last pale

wave, as autumn dies to bring

winter back, and then the spring,

we who die ourselves can peel

back another kind of veil

Step 3. Look for repeating patterns of wands and cups. When you see a pattern repeat, separate it with the edge symbol (|).

EXAMPLE: Poem scanned with wands, and cups, and edges in between each time the pattern /u repeats--showing its meter is trochaic tetrameter.

/ u| / u | /   u | /
In the season leaves should love,

/   u| /   u | / u| /
since it gives them leave to move

/   u| /   u | / u | /
through the wind, towards the ground

/   u | / u | /   u | /
they were watching while they hung,

/ u | /   u |/u| /
legend says there is a seam

/ u | / u | / u| /
stitching darkness like a name.

Finishing step 3: Name the meter, and add any finishing touches that are needed

EXAMPLE: Fully-scanned poem with finishing touches: marked with "ghost cups" to show the missing syllables of the last trochee of each line, and the "rest" showing the missing syllable of a trochee in the middle of line 3..

/ u | / u | /   u | / (u)
In the season leaves should love,

/   u | /   u | / u | / (u)
since it gives them leave to move

/   u | /   u | / u | / (u)
through the wind, towards the ground

/   u | / u | /   u | / (u)
they were watching while they hung,

/ u | /   u | / u | / (u)
legend says there is a seam

/ u | / u | / u | / (u)
stitching darkness like a name.

EXERCISE:

Copy the wands and cups you put before, and add the edges to this section of "Samhain." Finish by naming the meter, and adding any necessary finishing touches. Note: when you are adding the edges, you may notice something different in line 2. If you get confused putting in the edges starting at the beginning of the line, you can skip to the end of the line and put some edges in backwards from there. You should end up with one foot that's different from the base meter. This is fine! It's a common variation.

Now when dying grasses veil

earth from the sky in one last pale

wave, as autumn dies to bring

winter back, and then the spring,

we who die ourselves can peel

back another kind of veil

OK, now you are seriously scanning!

Before we move into the workbook part of this book, we will scan one more poem together.

THE HALF-WAND

This scansion will introduce our final scansion mark, the Half-Wand. If some syllables seem too strong to make acceptable cups, or too weak to make acceptable wands, you can consider marking them with a half-wand—a medium-level accent. Half-wands are the most subjective scansion tool, and some scanners don't use them at all—anything that's not a wand is simply a cup. To revisit a metaphor from the Accentuals chapter: if you are hearing *too* many half-wands, pour a little more water in the streambed and see which ones are still showing above the water. Those are the syllables you might promoting from cups to half-wands. It's best to follow the lead of the poet: some use a lot more half-wands than others, and many poets use none at all. Always check back in with the meaning-level: how will the half-wand add to a reader's understanding of the poem? (you can find conversations between Autumn Newman and myself discussing our scansion choices for this book in the

How to Scan a Poem audio recordings linked from the Poetry Witch Press website). If you use too many half-wands, they will become meaningless. So if you get confused, the basic rule of half-wands is, **when in doubt, don't**. After your wands are scanned, it's always a safe choice to scan all the remaining syllables as cups. Only use half-wands if you're sure. But when they are genuinely heard, they are priceless.

THE THREE-STEP METHOD, ONE MORE TIME

Step 1. Mark the accents with Wands.

EXAMPLE: Step 1. Lines with only the accented syllables (Wands) marked

/   /   /
I am the mother of sorrows,

  /   /   /
  I am the ender of grief;

/   /   /
I am the bud and the blossom,

  /   /   /
  I am the late-falling leaf.

  —Paul Laurence Dunbar

EXERCISE:

Add the Wands to this stanza of Dunbar's poem:

Come to me, brother, when weary,

Come when thy lonely heart swells;

I'll guide thy footsteps and lead thee

Down where the Dream Woman dwells.

Step 2. Mark the remaining syllables with Cups

EXAMPLE: Here is the opening of Dunbar's poem with both Wands and Cups marked.

/ u u / u u / u
I am the mother of sorrows,

  / u u / u u /
  I am the ender of grief;

/ u u / u u / u
I am the bud and the blossom,

  / u u / \ u /
  I am the late-falling leaf.

EXERCISE:

Copy the Wands you put before, and add Cups, on this stanza of Dunbar's poem:

Come to me, brother, when weary,

Come when thy lonely heart swells;

I'll guide thy footsteps and lead thee

Down where the Dream Woman dwells.

Step 3. Look for repeating patterns of Wands and Cups. When you see a pattern repeat, separate it with the Edge symbol (|).

EXAMPLE: Poem scanned with Wands, Cups, and edges, showing there are three dactyls in each line. There are variations at the ends of each line so that some lines end in a trochee and some in a single accent, instead of a full dactyl. Since both dactyl and trochee are *falling feet* (feet that fall from a stronger to weaker syllable (Wand to a Cup) they can easily be interchanged with each other without hurting the poem's rhythmic momentum.

/ u u | / u u | / u
I am the mother of sorrows,

/ u u | / u u | /
I am the ender of grief;

/ u u | / u u | / u
I am the bud and the blossom,

/ u u | / \ u | /
I am the late-falling leaf.

EXERCISE:
Copy the wands and cups you put before, and add edges to this stanza of Dunbar's poem:

Come to me, brother, when weary,

Come when thy lonely heart swells;

I'll guide thy footsteps and lead thee

Down where the Dream Woman dwells.

Finishing step 3: Name the meter, and add any finishing touches that are needed

EXAMPLE: Fully-scanned poem, showing its meter is dactylic trimeter, with finishing touches: marked as "ghost cups" to show the syllables of the third dactyl of each line.

/ u u | / u u | / u (u)
I am the mother of sorrows,

  / u u | / u u | / (u u)
  I am the ender of grief;

/ u u | / u u | / u (u)
I am the bud and the blossom,

  / u u | / \ u | / (u u)
  I am the late-falling leaf.

EXERCISE:

Copy the wands, cups, and edges you put before, and add needed finishing touches to this stanza of Dunbar's poem:

Come to me, brother, when weary,

Come when thy lonely heart swells;

I'll guide thy footsteps and lead thee

Down where the Dream Woman dwells.

Section 2

SCANSIONS

Now you have practiced all the basic tools of scansion, and you have already scanned three of the different meters included in this book: iambs, trochees, and dactyls. The rest of the book will guide you through poems to scan on your own, with a scanned version of each to check at the back of the book. (One difference between these scansions and those you will encounter "in the wild," of course, is that these are labelled in advance, so that you know what you are looking for. You will find some thoughts about this reality in the Afterword).

As you scan, savor how the process of scanning helps you appreciate each syllable of the poem and its particular, unique weight at this spot in the poem. Feel the delicious differences between lines that scan identically but have very different words. Feel the effects of any contrasts between your expectation and the actual pattern, as you move through the lines. This is the pleasure of scansion: it helps you to feel a poem's physical presence more attentively, more deeply, like taking part in a joyful dance of appreciation for the subtle beauties and deep complexities of a poem

PROCESS FOR DOING THE SCANSIONS

Start by reading some or all of the poem aloud.

Use a pencil with an eraser.

Follow Penny's Three-Step Method.

When doing wands, try the reverse-exaggeration method or the shout-across-the-room method, and remember you can use the dictionary for words of more than one syllable.

How to Scan a Poem

Read aloud often!

When in doubt, consult the Guiding Principles, and apply them *in order*.

When working with variations/substitutions, remember that falling and rising feet stick together. The only real exceptions are after line-breaks or strong caesuras. So the only place you are likely to find a trochee in an iambic poem, for example, is at the beginning of a line or after a midline punctuation mark or other strong pause. This makes common sense, as you will learn when you *read it aloud*!:)

As a general rule, every foot needs to have at least one wand (pyrrhics in iambic lines can be an exception, but they are usually followed by spondees or compensated for by an extra stress somewhere in the line).

Remember that beginnings and endings of lines can be quite a free-for-all zone. Don't be surprised if you find tailless lines (lines in falling meter missing one or two final cups), headless lines (lines in rising meter missing one or two beginning cups), or running starts (one or two extra cups at the beginning of lines in falling meter). Just mark anything that's missing or extra with ghost cups.

Check any scansion choice that feels unusual against the meaning of the words. How will this scansion choice affect the tone in which the words are said, the meaning of the line, and the meaning of the poem as a whole? If you are weighing two scansion choices, this can often be the deciding factor. It's a serious responsibility, a kind of energetic choice that can have wide implications. When in doubt, read aloud, and take all the time you need.

When you have a scansion you like, you can check it against the scansions in the back.

You will notice some of the scansions have quite a few half-wands, and others far fewer. This difference largely reflects the style of the individual poets. Some poets use a more tightly tuned string. Try to attune yourself to their sound.

Read the poems aloud again!

Enjoy!

POEMS TO SCAN

Cirilo F. Bautista
Trans. José Edmundo Ocampo Reyes

QUESTIONS AND ANSWERS

Don't you know that a mountain is nothing but smoke?

Don't you know that a thought is nothing but foam?

Don't you know that sackfuls of rice will go bad

when they're hidden deep down in the breast of a poem?

Make a dragon swoop down from a mountain of smoke

that your thoughts made of foam may be put to the test;

make a throne out of rice that's been kept in a nook

that a God may be wrought from the poem in your breast.

Sara Teasdale

I WOULD LIVE IN YOUR LOVE

I would live in your love as the sea-grasses live in the sea,

Borne up by each wave as it passes, drawn down by each wave that recedes;

I would empty my soul of the dreams that have gathered in me,

I would beat with your heart as it beats, I would follow your soul as it leads.

Annie Finch

KETTLE COVE

Through the upper and lower worlds, body and soul,

Through your softness and hardness, your wetness and roil,

May I rock in your mystery, speaking and whole,

Like the rockweeds You rock in your undersea coil!

You are fire in the rock and the water and wind,

in the earth and the sun and the ocean and air.

Like the rockweeds You rock in your undersea coil,

Half way between water and earth, I divide.

May I rock in your mystery, speaking and whole —

on your softness and hardness and wildness I ride!

In the center of sunlight, I am coming true!

In the pulling of ripples, I'm there!

I will answer your heart with me, my heart with You,

In this balance of waiting and air.

I am fire in the rock and the water and wind,

and the earth and the sun and the ocean and air.

On the point of the spray and the push of the tide,

I have rocked in your mystery, speaking and whole!

on your softness and hardness and wildness I ride

Like the rockweeds You rock, in your undersea coil.

Jeffrey Betcher

From WHISTLING THROUGH

1. DIAGNOSIS

Diagnosis is terminal. Life finds its shape

A few feet from the ground as it tries to take flight

In a fog of dead air, with a load of dead weight,

And a pilot who's just lost all feeling and sight.

I can hear the unknowable next whistling through …

… Through bright holes in a scan, through my fingers and bones,

Through the cracks in my plans … whistling right through.

It's the sound of a song I must sing, but don't know.

Life can syncopate: music, familiar but strange,

As the rhythm of spirit and flesh swells and fades,

Innuendo from angels that gravity waits

For this tangle of melody … death … to unbraid.

In the time it takes sunrise to free the day's light,

"It's not good news," can sum up the faint sounds of night.

2. WALL

"It's not good news" can sum up the faint sounds of night.

I can hear, over doctors and daylight, the noise

Of a half-life in pieces that's starting to rise

As through mud, like the pit from when I was a boy.

Dark release (now I know my death's "how," if not "when")

Seems to bubble up first, a blah-BLOOP in the room.

Then the ruckus of leaving my friends rocks my head

With a quiet as loud as when water breaks womb.

And then Wham! there's a wall, existential cement,

Staggered stones cut with questions and mortared with fate.

Life's no more than it seems, then we die, and then ... next?

If an answer exists, it comes one breath too late.

Prickly devils play tag on my neck's oily nape,

Between symptom and grave, as my life hangs agape.

3. MIND-FUCK

Between symptom and grave, as my life hangs agape,

Waits ba-RUM-bump, both wry and awry with it all.

So I cackle from fear ... out of turn, short of rage ...

As Absurdity's mind-fuck pins faith to the wall.

Ask philosopher, clergy, clinician alike:

Is it random, this cancer? Genetic? Bad luck?

Psychological sin or Pat Robertson tripe,

Like the backhand of God or creative self-fuck?

What a buttload of judgement I'm fighting today.

Anal tumors ... together as big as a cock ...

Up a gay guy? PuhLEASE! I don't fuck me that way.

And yet scrupulous ass answers tumorous knock.

It seems Death pulls on pants one gaunt leg at a time,

As my body is tricked, by itself, of its life.

Langston Hughes

DREAM VARIATIONS

To fling my arms wide

In some place of the sun,

To whirl and to dance

Till the white day is done.

Then rest at cool evening

Beneath a tall tree

While night comes on gently,

    Dark like me-

    That is my dream!

To fling my arms wide

In the face of the sun,

    Dance! Whirl! Whirl!

Till the quick day is done.

    Rest at pale evening…

A tall, slim tree…

    Night coming tenderly

    Black like me.

IAMBS TO SCAN

W. B. Yeats

WHEN YOU ARE OLD

When you are old and grey and full of sleep,

And nodding by the fire, take down this book,

And slowly read, and dream of the soft look

Your eyes had once, and of their shadows deep;

How many loved your moments of glad grace,

And loved your beauty with love false or true,

But one man loved the pilgrim soul in you,

And loved the sorrows of your changing face;

And bending down beside the glowing bars,

Murmur, a little sadly, how Love fled

And paced upon the mountains overhead

And hid his face amid a crowd of stars.

Annie Finch

EVE

When mother Eve took the first apple down

from the tree that grew where nature's heart had been

and came tumbling, circling, rosy, into sin,

which goddesses were lost, and which were found?

What spirals moved in pity and unwound

across our mother's body with the spin

of planets lost for us and all her kin?

What serpents curved their mouths into a frown,

but left their bodies twined in us like threads

that lead us back to her? Her presence warms,

and if I follow closely through the maze,

it is to where her remembered reaching spreads

in branching gifts, it is to her reaching arms

that I look, as if for something near to praise.

Frances Ellen Watkins Harper

BURY ME IN A FREE LAND

Make me a grave where'er you will,

In a lowly plain, or a lofty hill;

Make it among earth's humblest graves,

But not in a land where men are slaves.

I could not rest if around my grave

I heard the steps of a trembling slave;

His shadow above my silent tomb

Would make it a place of fearful gloom.

I could not rest if I heard the tread

Of a coffle gang to the shambles led,

And the mother's shriek of wild despair

Rise like a curse on the trembling air.

I could not sleep if I saw the lash

Drinking her blood at each fearful gash,

And I saw her babes torn from her breast,

Like trembling doves from their parent nest.

I'd shudder and start if I heard the bay

Of bloodhounds seizing their human prey,

And I heard the captive plead in vain

As they bound afresh his galling chain.

If I saw young girls from their mother's arms

Bartered and sold for their youthful charms,

My eye would flash with a mournful flame,

My death-paled cheek grow red with shame.

I would sleep, dear friends, where bloated might

Can rob no man of his dearest right;

My rest shall be calm in any grave

Where none can call his brother a slave.

I ask no monument, proud and high,

To arrest the gaze of the passers-by;

All that my yearning spirit craves,

Is bury me not in a land of slaves.

Hart Crane

From TO BROOKLYN BRIDGE

How many dawns, chill from his rippling rest

The seagull's wings shall dip and pivot him,

Shedding white rings of tumult, building high

Over the chained bay waters Liberty—

Then, with inviolate curve, forsake our eyes

As apparitional as sails that cross

Some page of figures to be filed away;

—Till elevators drop us from our day ...

I think of cinemas, panoramic sleights

With multitudes bent toward some flashing scene

Never disclosed, but hastened to again,

Foretold to other eyes on the same screen;

And Thee, across the harbor, silver paced

As though the sun took step of thee yet left

Some motion ever unspent in thy stride,—

Implicitly thy freedom staying thee!

Claude McKay

IF WE MUST DIE

If we must die—let it not be like hogs

Hunted and penned in an inglorious spot,

While round us bark the mad and hungry dogs,

Making their mock at our accursèd lot.

If we must die, O let us nobly die,

So that our precious blood may not be shed

In vain; then even the monsters we defy

Shall be constrained to honor us though dead!

O kinsmen! we must meet the common foe!

Though far outnumbered let us show us brave,

And for their thousand blows deal one death-blow!

What though before us lies the open grave?

Like men we'll face the murderous, cowardly pack,

Pressed to the wall, dying, but fighting back!

TROCHEES TO SCAN

Dorothy Parker

FIGHTING WORDS

Say my love is easy had,

    Say I'm bitten raw with pride,

Say I am too often sad,—

    Still behold me at your side.

Say I'm neither brave nor young,

    Say I woo and coddle care,

Say the devil touched my tongue,—

    Still you have my heart to wear.

But say my verses do not scan,

    And I get me another man!

Jessie Redmon Fauset

RAIN FUGUE

Slanting, driving, Summer rain

How you wash my heart of pain!

How you make me think of trees,

Ships and gulls and flashing seas!

In your furious, tearing wind,

Swells a chant that heals my mind;

And your passion high and proud,

Makes me shout and laugh aloud!

Autumn rains that start at dawn,

"Dropping veils of thinnest lawn,"

Soaking sod between dank grasses,

Sweeping golden leaves in masses,—

Blotting, blurring out the Past,

In a dream you hold me fast;

Calling, coaxing to forget

Things that are, for things not yet.

Winter tempest, winter rain,

Hurtling down with might and main,

You but make me hug my hearth,

Laughing, sheltered from your wrath.

Now I woo my dancing fire,

Piling, piling drift-wood higher.

Books and friends and pictures old,

Hearten while you pound and scold!

Pattering, wistful showers of Spring

Set me to remembering

Far-off times and lovers too,

Gentle joys and heart-break rue,—

Memories I'd as lief forget,

Were not oblivion sadder yet.

Ah! you twist my mind with pain,

Wistful, whispering April rain!

Summer, Autumn, Winter rain,

How you ease my heart of pain!

Whispering, wistful showers of Spring,

How I love the hurt you bring!

Henry Wadsworth Longfellow

From THE SONG OF HIAWATHA

Thus it was that in the North-land

After that unheard-of coldness,

That intolerable Winter,

Came the Spring with all its splendor,

All its birds and all its blossoms,

All its flowers and leaves and grasses.

Sailing on the wind to northward,

Flying in great flocks, like arrows,

Like huge arrows shot through heaven,

Passed the swan, the Mahnahbezee,

Speaking almost as a man speaks;

And in long lines waving, bending

Like a bow-string snapped asunder,

Came the white goose, Waw-be-wawa;

And in pairs, or singly flying,

Mahng the loon, with clangorous pinions,

The blue heron, the Shuh-shuh-gah,

And the grouse, the Mushkodasa.

In the thickets and the meadows

Piped the bluebird, the Owaissa,

On the summit of the lodges

Sang the robin, the Opechee,

In the covert of the pine-trees

Cooed the pigeon, the Omemee;

Annie Finch

SAMHAIN
October 31

In the season leaves should love,

since it gives them leave to move

through the wind, towards the ground

they were watching while they hung,

legend says there is a seam

stitching darkness like a name.

Now when dying grasses veil

earth from the sky in one last pale

wave, as autumn dies to bring

winter back, and then the spring,

we who die ourselves can peel

back another kind of veil

that hangs among us like thick smoke.

Tonight at last I feel it shake.

I feel the nights stretching away

thousands long behind the days,

till they reach the darkness where

all of me is ancestor.

I turn my hand and feel a touch

move with me, and when I brush

my young mind across another,

I have met my mother's mother.

Sure as footsteps in my waiting

self, I find her, and she brings

arms that hold answers for me,

intimate, waiting, bounty:

"Carry me." She leaves this trail

through a shudder of the veil,

and leaves, like amber where she stays,

a gift for her perpetual gaze.

William Stanley Braithwaite

A SEA-PRAYER

LORD of wind and water

Where the ships go down

Reaching to the sunrise,

Lifting like a crown,

Out of the deep-hidden

Wells of night and day —

Mind the great sea-farers

On the open way.

When the last lights darken

On the far coastline,

Wave and port and peril

Sea-Lord — all are thine.

William Blake

THE TYGER

Tyger Tyger, burning bright,

In the forests of the night;

What immortal hand or eye,

Could frame thy fearful symmetry?

In what distant deeps or skies.

Burnt the fire of thine eyes?

On what wings dare he aspire?

What the hand, dare seize the fire?

And what shoulder, & what art,

Could twist the sinews of thy heart?

And when thy heart began to beat.

What dread hand? & what dread feet?

What the hammer? what the chain,

In what furnace was thy brain?

What the anvil? what dread grasp.

Dare its deadly terrors clasp?

When the stars threw down their spears

And water'd heaven with their tears:

Did he smile his work to see?

Did he who made the Lamb make thee?

Tyger Tyger, burning bright,

In the forests of the night;

What immortal hand or eye,

Dare frame thy fearful symmetry?

DACTYLICS TO SCAN

Autumn Newman

SHEDDING SKIN

This is a thunderclap splitting the silence.

This is the lightning bolt thrown.

This is a pain like you could not give to me.

This is the hollow in stone.

This is too seismic, unsteady and sudden.

This is the cracking of bone.

This is a breath that is drenched in the sacred.

This is the rain alone.

This is my body, a flower burst open.

This is the color I've grown.

Paul Laurence Dunbar

THE PARADOX

I am the mother of sorrows,

I am the ender of grief;

I am the bud and the blossom,

I am the late-falling leaf.

I am thy priest and thy poet,

I am thy serf and thy king;

I cure the tears of the heartsick,

When I come near they shall sing.

White are my hands as the snowdrop;

Swart are my fingers as clay;

Dark is my frown as the midnight,

Fair is my brow as the day.

Battle and war are my minions,

Doing my will as divine;

I am the calmer of passions,

Peace is a nursling of mine.

Speak to me gently or curse me,

Seek me or fly from my sight;

I am thy fool in the morning,

Thou art my slave in the night.

Down to the grave will I take thee,

Out from the noise of the strife;

Then shalt thou see me and know me—

Death, then, no longer, but life.

Then shalt thou sing at my coming,

Kiss me with passionate breath,

Clasp me and smile to have thought me

Aught save the foeman of Death.

Come to me, brother, when weary,

Come when thy lonely heart swells;

I'll guide thy footsteps and lead thee

Down where the Dream Woman dwells.

Elizabeth Akers Allen

ROCK ME TO SLEEP

Backward, turn backward, O Time, in your flight,

Make me a child again just for tonight!

Mother, come back from the echoless shore,

Take me again to your heart as of yore;

Kiss from my forehead the furrows of care,

Smooth the few silver threads out of my hair;

Over my slumbers your loving watch keep;—

Rock me to sleep, mother, – rock me to sleep!

Backward, flow backward, O tide of the years!

I am so weary of toil and of tears,—

Toil without recompense, tears all in vain,—

Take them, and give me my childhood again!

I have grown weary of dust and decay,—

Weary of flinging my soul-wealth away

Weary of sowing for others to reap;—

Rock me to sleep, mother – rock me to sleep!

Tired of the hollow, the base, the untrue,

Mother, O mother, my heart calls for you!

Many a summer the grass has grown green,

Blossomed and faded, our faces between:

Yet, with strong yearning and passionate pain,

Long I tonight for your presence again.

Come from the silence so long and so deep;—

Rock me to sleep, mother, – rock me to sleep!

Over my heart, in the days that are flown,

No love like mother-love ever has shone;

No other worship abides and endures,—

Faithful, unselfish, and patient like yours:

None like a mother can charm away pain

From the sick soul and the world-weary brain.

Slumber's soft calms o'er my heavy lids creep;—

Rock me to sleep, mother, – rock me to sleep!

Come, let your brown hair, just lighted with gold,

Fall on your shoulders again as of old;

Let it drop over my forehead tonight,

Shading my faint eyes away from the light;

For with its sunny-edged shadows once more

Haply will throng the sweet visions of yore;

Lovingly, softly, its bright billows sweep;—

Rock me to sleep, mother, – rock me to sleep!

Mother, dear mother, the years have been long

Since I last listened your lullaby song:

Sing, then, and unto my soul it shall seem

Womanhood's years have been only a dream.

Clasped to your heart in a loving embrace,

With your light lashes just sweeping my face,

Never hereafter to wake or to weep;—

Rock me to sleep, mother, – rock me to sleep!

A. E. Stallings

ARACHNE GIVES THANKS TO ATHENA

It is no punishment. They are mistaken –

The brothers, the father. My prayers were answered.

I was all fingertips. Nothing was perfect:

What I had woven, the moths will have eaten;

At the end of my rope was a noose's knot.

Now it's no longer the thing, but the pattern,

And that will endure, even though webs be broken.

I, if not beautiful, am beauty's maker.

Old age cannot rob me, nor cowardly lovers.

The moon once pulled blood from me. Now I pull silver.

Here are the lines I pulled from my own belly –

Hang them with rainbows, ice, dewdrops, darkness.

Thomas Hardy

THE VOICE

Woman much missed, how you call to me, call to me,

Saying that now you are not as you were

When you had changed from the one who was all to me,

But as at first, when our day was fair.

Can it be you that I hear? Let me view you, then,

Standing as when I drew near to the town

Where you would wait for me: yes, as I knew you then,

Even to the original air-blue gown!

Or is it only the breeze, in its listlessness

Traveling across the wet mead to me here,

You being ever dissolved to wan wistlessness,

Heard no more again far or near?

    Thus I; faltering forward,

    Leaves around me falling,

Wind oozing thin through the thorn from norward,

    And the woman calling.

AMPHIBRACHS TO SCAN

Annie Finch

MY SISTER WHO KEPT HER ABORTION A SECRET

My sister — the daring, the rider, the dancer —

Whose silence put her in the path of this danger —

Is breaking the heart of my question or answer

Again, as she moves off to death, like a stranger.

She's spun herself on. And the poisons that filled her?

The secret that fed her? Those heart-heavy chances

Her life stole and killed until, finally, they spilled her

Out through the universe? Those were her dances.

No mother has held her — No village will mourn her —

No ritual frames her —Come, help me reclaim her —

Her body won't bear her again — nor be borne. Her

true name is no secret — and — we will not blame her.

My sister, the daring, the rider, the dancer

Who steps out, who stepped in the path of the danger.

Anna Lena Phillips Bell

HONEYSUCKLE

For scant weeks in spring when the ground has had time to get warmer,

and all the white flowers whose forms are so hard to imagine

are coming to bloom, and the air smells each day of some newness,

a sweetness whose name, like the scent, flags the tip of the tongue

then leaves, leads me onward, leads bees on, leads moths, leads small flies

(for who knows which beast every flower is meant to attract

and who can collect each one's name?), I breathe in as much of

the air as will flow through my lungs before—sudden, persistent—

you lower down over the piedmont, imparting a one-noted

sweetness that has to content us all summer, for only

a rare other fragrance can cut through those curtains of sugar.

Samuel Woodworth
THE OLD OAKEN BUCKET

How dear to this heart are the scenes of my childhood,

When fond recollection presents them to view!

The orchard, the meadow, the deep-tangled wild-wood,

And every loved spot that my infancy knew!

The wide-spreading pond, and the mill that stood by it,

The bridge, and the rock where the cataract fell,

The cot of my father, the dairy-house nigh it,

And e'en the rude bucket that hung in the well—

The old oaken bucket, the iron-bound bucket,

The moss-covered bucket which hung in the well.

That moss covered bucket I hailed as a treasure,

For often at noon, when return'd from the field,

I found it the source of an exquisite pleasure,

The purest and sweetest that nature can yield.

How ardent I seized it, with hands that were glowing,

And quick to the white pebbled bottom it fell

Then soon, with the emblem of truth o'erflowing,

And dripping with coolness, it rose from the well.

How sweet from the green, mossy brim to receive it,

As, poised on the curb, it inclined to my lips!

Not a full blushing goblet could tempt me to leave it,

Tho' filled with the nectar that Jupiter sips.

And now, far removed from the loved habitation,

The tear of regret will intrusively swell,

As fancy reverts to my father's plantation,

And sighs for the bucket that hung in the well.

Austin Allen

THERE ONCE WAS

A tango that's also a waltz—

A rhythm that awkwardly halts,

But sways a few hearers

In old barroom mirrors

That say every form has its faults.

*

There once was a gentleman listed

Among those who never existed.

His colleagues politely

Reminded him nightly—

He woke in a sweat and persisted.

I leaf through a yellowing tome.

They must have retired the gloam

In, what, 1910?

Only twilight since then.

I'm homesick for when I missed home.

There once was a State Representative

Who feared that her base would resent it if

She didn't erase

Both herself and her base.

Till autumn, the plan remained tentative.

I speak out. I feel that I must.

I hear my own spiel with disgust.

I see others make

My egregious mistake.

I speak out. I feel that I must.

The gesture, the comment, the eyeroll—

The germ of a fury gone viral—

The long, glowing dream

Of a scroll or a stream

That seems to twist into a spiral . . .

The ocelot gazed like a tourist.

No monkeys or parakeets chorused.

Fresh radio beats

Floated over the streets

Of the precinct that once was a forest.

The news is the usual crap—

I sigh and lie down for a nap.

Your body and eyes

Repossess me ... I rise.

A town's disappeared from the map.

Come back while the woods are still wild,

Come back without mortgage or child,

Come riding my way

When the climate in May

Agrees, for one night, to be mild.

There once was a time and a place

Shaved down to the ghost of a trace

Of a scholarly laugh

How to Scan a Poem

In the last paragraph

Of a note on an ode to a vase.

I'm losing the thread of my thesis.

I once said out loud to my niece's

Beloved stuffed penguin,

Whose smile is so sanguine:

"Your whole fucking pole is in pieces."

They're fighting a war overseas;

We can't seem to locate our keys;

A column's been slaughtered;

Our plants are unwatered;

Our windshield's beginning to freeze.

There once was a girl at the border.

Her papers were squarely in order.

The quieter guard

Started staring too hard.

There once was a girl at the border.

There once was a noble intent,

A clean breeze, a stabilized rent,

The passenger pigeon,

My grandmother's kitchen,

Aretha, Pangaea, your scent . . .

There once was a civilization

Whose peak was of modest duration.

An upside-down spire

Juts out of the mire,

Which bubbles a long exhalation.

Anna Akhmatova

LOT'S WIFE

"But his wife looked back from behind him, and she became a pillar of salt."
— Genesis 19:25-26

The righteous man followed where God's angel guide

shone on through black mountains, imposing and bright—

but pain tore his wife's breast. It turned her aside

and said, "Look again! There is time for one sight

Of towers, and Sodom's red halls, and the place

Where you sang in the courtyard or wove on your loom

By windows now empty—where you knew the embrace

Of love with your husband—where birth filled the room—."

She looked. And the sight was more bitter than pain.

It shut up her eyes so she saw nothing more;

She shimmered to salt; her feet moved in vain,

Deep rooted at last in the place she died for.

Who weeps for her now? Who can care for the fate

Of someone like that—a mere unhappy wife?

My heart will remember. I carry the weight

Of one who looked back, though it cost her her life.

DIPODICS, ETC. TO SCAN

Robert Frost

FOR ONCE, THEN, SOMETHING

Others taunt me with having knelt at well-curbs

Always wrong to the light, so never seeing

Deeper down in the well than where the water

Gives me back in a shining surface picture

Me myself in the summer heaven godlike

Looking out of a wreath of fern and cloud puffs.

Once, when trying with chin against a well-curb,

I discerned, as I thought, beyond the picture,

Through the picture, a something white, uncertain,

Something more of the depths—and then I lost it.

Water came to rebuke the too clear water.

One drop fell from a fern, and lo, a ripple

Shook whatever it was lay there at bottom,

Blurred it, blotted it out. What was that whiteness?

Truth? A pebble of quartz? For once, then, something.

John Masefield

SEA FEVER

I must go down to the seas again, to the lonely sea and the sky,

And all I ask is a tall ship and a star to steer her by,

And the wheel's kick and the wind's song and the white sail's shaking,

And a grey mist on the sea's face, and a grey dawn breaking.

I must go down to the seas again, for the call of the running tide

Is a wild call and a clear call that may not be denied;

And all I ask is a windy day with the white clouds flying,

And the flung spray and the blown spume, and the sea-gulls crying.

I must go down to the seas again, to the vagrant gypsy life,

To the gull's way and the whale's way, where the wind's like a whetted knife;

And all I ask is a merry yarn from a laughing fellow-rover,

And quiet sleep and a sweet dream when the long trick's over.

Edgar Allan Poe

from THE RAVEN

Once upon a midnight dreary, while I pondered weak and weary,

Over many a quaint and curious volume of forgotten lore,

While I nodded, nearly napping, suddenly there came a tapping,

As of some one gently rapping, rapping at my chamber door.

`'Tis some visitor,' I muttered, `tapping at my chamber door -

Only this, and nothing more.'

Ah, distinctly I remember it was in the bleak December,

And each separate dying ember wrought its ghost upon the floor.

Eagerly I wished the morrow; - vainly I had sought to borrow

From my books surcease of sorrow - sorrow for the lost Lenore -

For the rare and radiant maiden whom the angels name Lenore -

Nameless here for evermore.

And the silken sad uncertain rustling of each purple curtain

Thrilled me - filled me with fantastic terrors never felt before;

So that now, to still the beating of my heart, I stood repeating

`'Tis some visitor entreating entrance at my chamber door -

Some late visitor entreating entrance at my chamber door; -

This it is, and nothing more,'

Presently my soul grew stronger; hesitating then no longer,

`Sir,' said I, `or Madam, truly your forgiveness I implore;

But the fact is I was napping, and so gently you came rapping,

And so faintly you came tapping, tapping at my chamber door,

That I scarce was sure I heard you' - here I opened wide the door; -

Darkness there, and nothing more.

Deep into that darkness peering, long I stood there wondering, fearing,

Doubting, dreaming dreams no mortal ever dared to dream before;

But the silence was unbroken, and the darkness gave no token,

And the only word there spoken was the whispered word, `Lenore!'

This I whispered, and an echo murmured back the word, `Lenore!'

Merely this and nothing more.

SCANNED POEMS

Anonymous

THIRTY DAYS HATH SEPTEMBER Accentual

 / / / /
April, June and November
 / /   / /
All the rest have thirty-one
  / /   / /
Save February, and it alone,
   /   / / /
Has twenty-eight we do confine
  /   /   /   /
Till Leap Year gives it twenty nine.

Annie Finch

ANOTHER RELUCTANCE Accentual

 /   /   / /
Chestnuts fell in the charred season,
/ /   /   /
fell finally, finding room
 / /   / /
in air to open their old cases

         /   /   /   /
so they gleam out from the gold leaves
         /   /   /   /
in the dust now, where they dropped down.

  /   /   /   /
I go watch them, waiting for winter,
       /   /   /   /
Their husks open and holding on.
       /   /   /   /
Those rusted rims are rigid-hard
       /   /   /   /
And cling clean to the clear brown.
       /   / /   /
But the fall sun sinks soon

            /   /   /   /
And the day draws to its dark end,
       /   /   /   /
And the feet give up the gray walk,
 /   /   /   /
No longer lingering, light gone.
       /   /   /   /
And I am here and do not go home.

   /   /   /   /
Hollow gifts to cold children:
       /   /   /   /
The chestnuts they hid in small caches

　　　　/　/　　　　　　/　　/
have gone hollow, their grain gone,

　　　　/　　/　　　　　/　　　　　/
their gleam gone, and the children are home.

Edna St. Vincent Millay

RECUERDO   Accentual

　/　　　　　/　/　　　　/
We were very tired, we were very merry—

　　　　/　　　　　　/　　/　　　　　/
We had gone back and forth all night on the ferry.

　　　/　　　/　　　　　/　　　　/
It was bare and bright, and smelled like a stable—

　　　　/　　　　　/　　　　/　　　　　/
But we looked into a fire, we leaned across a table,

　　/　　　/　　　/　　　　/
We lay on a hill-top underneath the moon;

　　　　/　　　　　/　　　　　　/　　　　/
And the whistles kept blowing, and the dawn came soon.

　/　　　　　/　/　　　　/
We were very tired, we were very merry—

　　　　/　　　　　/　　/　　　　　/
We had gone back and forth all night on the ferry.

　　/　　　/　　　　/　　　/
And you ate an apple, and I ate a pear,

　　　　/　　　/　　　　　/　　　　/

From a dozen of each we had bought somewhere;

      /   /   /   /

And the sky went wan, and the wind came cold,

     /   /   /   /

And the sun rose dripping, a bucketful of gold.

/   / /   /

We were very tired, we were very merry—

    /   /   /   /

We had gone back and forth all night on the ferry.

       /   /   /   /

We hailed, "Good morrow, mother!" to a shawl-covered head,

  /   /   /   /

And bought a morning paper, which neither of us read;

   /   /   /   /

And she wept, "God bless you!" for the apples and pears,

   /   /   /   /

And we gave her all our money but our subway fares.

Cirilo F. Bautista
Trans. José Edmundo Ocampo Reyes

QUESTIONS AND ANSWERS　　**Anapestic tetrameter**

u   u / |u u / | u u /|u u /
Don't you know that a mountain is nothing but smoke?

u   u / |u u / |u /|u u /
Don't you know that a thought is nothing but foam?

u   u / |u / |u u / |u u /
Don't you know that sackfuls of rice will go bad

```
u    u    / | u  \   /   | u  u   /   | u u /
```
when they're hidden deep down in the breast of a poem?

```
u    u / | u  u      /   | u  u / | u   u /
```
Make a dragon swoop down from a mountain of smoke
```
u    u   /      | u    u  /  | u   u  /  | u u /
```
that your thoughts made of foam may be put to the test;
```
u   u  /   | u u / | u    u    /  | u u /
```
make a throne out of rice that's been kept in a nook
```
u  u / | u  u   /       | u    u   /   | u  u   /
```
that a God may be wrought from the poem in your breast.

Sara Teasdale

I WOULD LIVE IN YOUR LOVE   **Anapestic pentameter and hexameter**

```
u u    / | u  u    /   | u  u / | u   u    / | u u /
```
I would live in your love as the sea-grasses live in the sea,
```
u       / | u  u     /     | u u / | u   u    / | u  u    / | u   u  /
```
Borne up by each wave as it passes, drawn down by each wave that recedes;

```
u u    / | u  u   / | u u  /   | u   u     / | u  u /
```
I would empty my soul of the dreams that have gathered in me,
```
u  u     / | u  u   /  | u u / | u u   / | u   u /
```
I would beat with your heart as it beats, I would follow your soul
```
u  u /
```
as it leads.

Annie Finch

KETTLE COVE   **Anapestic tetrameter**

```
u    u  / | u  u  / | u  u   / | u  u  /
```
Through the upper and lower worlds, body and soul,
```
u      u  / | u  u  / | u    u  / | u  u  /
```
Through your softness and hardness, your wetness and roil,
```
u u / | u u  / | u u   / | u  u  /
```
May I rock in your mystery, speaking and whole,
```
u    u  / | \    u  /  | u  u  / | u u  /
```
Like the rockweeds You rock in your undersea coil!

```
u  u  / | u u  / | u  u  / | u u  /
```
You are fire in the rock and the water and wind,
```
u u  /  | u  u  / | u  u  / | u  u  /
```
in the earth and the sun and the ocean and air.

```
u    u  / | \    u  /  | u  u  / | u u  /
```
Like the rockweeds You rock in your undersea coil,
```
u   / | u   u  / | u u   /  | u u /
```
Half way between water and earth, I divide.
```
u  u / | u  u  / | u u   / | u   u   /
```
May I rock in your mystery, speaking and whole —
```
u  u  / | u  u  / | u   u  / | u  u  /
```
on your softness and hardness and wildness I ride!

```
u u  / | u  u / | /   u  u | /  u   \
```
In the center of sunlight, I am coming true!
```
u  u  / | u   u  / | u   u   /
```
In the pulling of ripples, I'm there!

u u / | u u   / | u u / | u   u   /
I will answer your heart with me, my heart with You,
u u / | u u / | u u /
In this balance of waiting and air.

u u / | u u / | u u / | u   u /
I am fire in the rock and the water and wind,
 u u / | u u / | u u / | u   u /
and the earth and the sun and the ocean and air.

u u / | u u / | u u / | u u /
On the point of the spray and the push of the tide,
u u / | u u / | u u / | u   u /
I have rocked in your mystery, speaking and whole!
u   u   / | u   u   / | u   u   / | u   u   /
on your softness and hardness and wildness I ride
u   u   / | \   u / | u u   / | u u /
Like the rockweeds You rock, in your undersea coil.

Jeffrey Betcher

From WHISTLING THROUGH   Anapestic tetrameter

1. Diagnosis
 \ u / | u u / | u u / | u   u   /
Diagnosis is terminal. Life finds its shape
u \   / | u   u   / | u u / | u u /
A few feet from the ground as it tries to take flight
u u / | u \   / | u u / | u \   /
In a fog of dead air, with a load of dead weight,

u u /|u u   / |u u /|u u   /
And a pilot who's just lost all feeling and sight.
u   u   / |u   u /|u u   / | \ u   /
I can hear the unknowable next whistling through …
         u   \   / |u u / |u   u   /|u u   /
… Through bright holes in a scan, through my fingers and bones,
u   u / |u u / |#   / |u   u   /
Through the cracks in my plans … whistling right through.
u   u   / |u u / |u u   / | u   u   /
It's the sound of a song I must sing, but don't know.
\ u   /| u   u   /| u   u /|u u   /
Life can syncopate: music, familiar but strange,
u u   / | u   u /|u u   / | \   u   /
As the rhythm of spirit and flesh swells and fades,
u u /|u   u   /|u   u /|u u   /
Innuendo from angels that gravity waits
u   u   / |u   u /|u u   / | u u   /
For this tangle of melody … death … to unbraid.
u   u   / |u u   / |u u / |u   u   /
In the time it takes sunrise to free the day's light,
u   u   / | \   u   / |u u / | \   u   /
"It's not good news," can sum up the faint sounds of night.

2. Wall

  u   u   / | \   u   / |u u / | \   u   /
"It's not good news" can sum up the faint sounds of night.
u u   / | \ u / |u   u   / |u   u   /
I can hear, over doctors and daylight, the noise
u u /| u u / |u   u   / |u u   /
Of a half-life in pieces that's starting to rise

u u   / | u u / | u   u   / | u u   /
As through mud, like the pit from when I was a boy.
u   u / | u   u / | u u   / | u u   /
Dark release (now I know my death's "how," if not "when")
u   u / | u u / | u u   / | u u   /
Seems to bubble up first, a blah-BLOOP in the room.
u   u / | u u / | u u   / | u   u   /
Then the ruckus of leaving my friends rocks my head
u   u / | u u / | u   u   / | u u   /
With a quiet as loud as when water breaks womb.
u   u   / | u   u / | u u / | u u   /
And then Wham! there's a wall, existential cement,
 /   u   / | /   u   / | u u   / | u   u   /
Staggered stones cut with questions and mortared with fate.
u   u   / | u   u / | u   u / | u u   /
Life's no more than it seems, then we die, and then ... next?
u u / | u u / | u \   / | /   u   /
If an answer exists, it comes one breath too late.
 / u   / | u   /   / | u u   / | u u   /
Prickly devils play tag on my neck's oily nape,
u   u   / | u   u   / | u u / | \   u /
Between symptom and grave, as my life hangs agape.

3. Mind-Fuck

u   u   / | u   u   / | u u / | \   u /
Between symptom and grave, as my life hangs agape,
u   u   / | /   /   / | u u / | u u /
Waits ba-RUM-bump, both wry and awry with it all.
u u / | u u   / | u u / | u   u   /
So I cackle from fear ... out of turn, short of rage ...

```
u  u  / |u u   /  |   / /   /  |u u   /
```
As Absurdity's mind-fuck pins faith to the wall.
```
 u    u  /|u u   / |u    u /|u u  /
```
Ask philosopher, clergy, clinician alike:
```
u u / | u   u  / | u   u /| u   u   /
```
Is it random, this cancer? Genetic? Bad luck?
```
u   u /|u u   / |u  u  /|u u    /
```
Psychological sin or Pat Robertson tripe,
```
 u   u    / |  u   u   /  |u u /|u  u    /
```
Like the backhand of God or creative self-fuck?
```
u    u / | u   u  / | u    u  / | u    u  /
```
What a buttload of judgement I'm fighting today.
```
(/) u   /  | u      u / | u u  /  | u u   /
```
Anal tumors … together as big as a cock …
```
u   u  / | u    u    /    | u u   /  | u u    /
```
Up a gay guy? PuhLEASE! I don't fuck me that way.
```
u    u / | u u    /  | /\ u    / | u u    /
```
And yet scrupulous ass answers tumorous knock.
```
u   u    /   | u   u  /  | u    u    / | u u  /
```
It seems Death pulls on pants one gaunt leg at a time,
```
 u    u  / |u u   /      | u  u  / | u u   /
```
As my body is tricked, by itself, of its life.

Langston Hughes

DREAM VARIATIONS   **Anapestic dimeter**

```
u  /  | u   u   /
```
To fling my arms wide
```
u   u   /  | u u   /
```
In some place of the sun,

u / | u u /
To whirl and to dance
u u / | \ u /
Till the white day is done.
u / | u u / (u u)
Then rest at cool evening
u / | u u /
Beneath a tall tree
u / | u u / (u)
While night comes on gently,
(u u) / | u /
    Dark like me-
(u u) / | u u /
    That is my dream!

u / | u u /
To fling my arms wide
u u / | u u /
In the face of the sun,
(u u) / | / /
    Dance! Whirl! Whirl!
u u / | u u /
Till the quick day is done.
(u u) / | u u / (u u)
    Rest at pale evening…
u / | u /
A tall, slim tree…
(u u) / | \ u / (u u)
    Night coming tenderly
(u u) / | u /
    Black like me.

W. B. Yeats

WHEN YOU ARE OLD   Iambic pentameter

```
u    /  | u  / | u  /  | u  / | u  /
```
When you are old and grey and full of sleep,
```
u   /  | u  / | u   / |  /   u   | u  /
```
And nodding by the fire, take down this book,
```
u    / | u  /  | u  /   | u  u | /   /
```
And slowly read, and dream of the soft look
```
u    /  |  /  /   | u  u | u  /  | u   /
```
Your eyes had once, and of their shadows deep;

```
u   / | u  /  | u   /  | u  u | /   /
```
How many loved your moments of glad grace,
```
u    /  | u   / | u  u | /   /  | u  /
```
And loved your beauty with love false or true,
```
u   /  |  /  /  | u  /  | u  /  | u  /
```
But one man loved the pilgrim soul in you,
```
u   /  | u  /  | u  u | u   /  | u   /
```
And loved the sorrows of your changing face;

```
u   / | u   /  | u  /  | u  /  | u   /
```
And bending down beside the glowing bars,
```
/    u  | u  / | u  / | u   /  |  /   /
```
Murmur, a little sadly, how Love fled
```
u   /   | u  / | u   /  | u   / | u  /
```
And paced upon the mountains overhead
```
u    /  | u   / | u  / | u   /  | u  /
```
And hid his face amid a crowd of stars.

Annie Finch

EVE   **Iambic pentameter**

```
u   / | u   / | u  u | /   / | u  /
```
When mother Eve took the first apple down
```
u  u  / | u  /  | u   / | u   / | u  /
```
from the tree that grew where nature's heart had been
```
u  u   / | u    / | u  / | u  / | u  /
```
and came tumbling, circling, rosy, into sin,
```
u   / | u / | u   / | u  /  | u   /
```
which goddesses were lost, and which were found?
```
u    / | u  /  | u  / | u  / | u  /
```
What spirals moved in pity and unwound
```
u / | u  / | u   / | u   /  | u  /
```
across our mother's body with the spin
```
u / | u   / | u  / | u  / | u  /
```
of planets lost for us and all her kin?
```
u    / | u    /  | u  /   | \ / | u  /
```
What serpents curved their mouths into a frown,
```
u  / | u   / | u   /  | u  / | u  /
```
but left their bodies twined in us like threads
```
u   / | u  / | u / | u   / | u  /
```
that lead us back to her? Her presence warms,
```
u  / | u / | u   / | u   /   | u  /
```
and if I follow closely through the maze,
```
u / | u  /  | u  u  / | u   / | u  /
```
it is to where her remembered reaching spreads
```
u  / | u    / | u u / | u  / | u  /
```
in branching gifts, it is to her reaching arms
```
u  u  /  | u  / | u  / | u   /  | u  /
```
that I look, as if for something near to praise.

Frances Ellen Watkins Harper

BURY ME IN A FREE LAND **Iambic tetrameter**

/   u | u / | u \ | u /
Make me a grave where'er you will,

u u / | u / | u u / | u /
In a lowly plain, or a lofty hill;

/   u | u / | /   / | u /
Make it among earth's humblest graves,

u   / | u u / | u   / | u /
But not in a land where men are slaves.

u / | u / | u u / | u /
I could not rest if around my grave

u / | u / | u u / | u /
I heard the steps of a trembling slave;

u   / | u u / | u / | u /
His shadow above my silent tomb

u   / | u u / | u / | u /
Would make it a place of fearful gloom.

u / | u / | u u / | u   /
I could not rest if I heard the tread

u u / | u / | u u / | u /
Of a coffle gang to the shambles led,

u   u / | u / | u / | u /
And the mother's shriek of wild despair

/   u | u / | u u   / | u /
Rise like a curse on the trembling air.

```
/  \   | \   /    |u u  / | u   /
```
I could not sleep if I saw the lash
```
 /    u  |u   /    |u  u    /| u   /
```
Drinking her blood at each fearful gash,
```
u   u  / | u   /  |  /   /   \  | u  /
```
And I saw her babes torn from her breast,
```
u    /  | u    /  | u   u   / | u  /
```
Like trembling doves from their parent nest.

```
 u   / |u   u   / |u u  /  | u   /
```
I'd shudder and start if I heard the bay
```
u   /  |  u    / | u  u   / | u   /
```
Of bloodhounds seizing their human prey,
```
u   u  /   | u    /| u   /   | u   /
```
And I heard the captive plead in vain
```
u   u    /   | u / | u   / | u   /
```
As they bound afresh his galling chain.

```
u u /  | u     /  | u   u   / | u   /
```
If I saw young girls from their mother's arms,
```
 /    u  | u   / |u  u   / | u   /
```
Bartered and sold for their youthful charms,
```
u   /  | u    /  | u  u  / | u   /
```
My eye would flash with a mournful flame,
```
u    /   |  \    /  | \   /  | u   /
```
My death-paled cheek grow red with shame.

```
u   u    /  | u   /    | u    / | u   /
```
I would sleep, dear friends, where bloated might
```
u   /  | u   /  |u  u  / | u   /
```
Can rob no man of his dearest right;

How to Scan a Poem

u / | u   u   / | u / | u   /
My rest shall be calm in any grave
u   / | u / | u / | u u /
Where none can call his brother a slave.

u / | u   / | u u   / | u   /
I ask no monument, proud and high,
u   u / | u   / | u u / | u   /
To arrest the gaze of the passers-by;
/   u | u   / | u   / | u   /
All that my yearning spirit craves,
u / | u u / | u u / | u   /
Is bury me not in a land of slaves.

Hart Crane

TO BROOKLYN BRIDGE   **Iambic pentameter**

/   \ | u   / | /   \ | u   / | u   /
How many dawns, chill from his rippling rest,
 u   / | /   / | u   / | u   / | u   /
The seagull's wings shall dip and pivot him,
/ u | /   / | u / | u   / | u   /
Shedding white rings of tumult, building high
 / u | u   /   u / | u / | u / | u   / | u   /
/ u | u   / | /   / / | u / | u /
Over the chained bay waters Liberty—

```
  /   u  |u /|u  u  /  |  u  /|  u   /
```
Then, with inviolate curve, forsake our eyes
```
   u  /| u /|u /| u  /  |  u    /
```
As apparitional as sails that cross
```
    /   /|  u  /| u  u|  u  /| u   /
```
Some page of figures to be filed away;
```
    \ /|u /|u     /| \  /|  u   /
```
—Till elevators drop us from our day ...

```
  u   /| u /|u  u  /  |u  /|u   /
```
I think of cinemas, panoramic sleights
```
   u  /| u  /|  /   /   | u   /| u  /
```
With multitudes bent toward some flashing scene
```
  / u|  u  /  |  u   /| u  /|u /
```
Never disclosed, but hastened to again,
```
  u   /|   u  /|u  /  |  u  u|  /   /
```
Foretold to other eyes on the same screen;

```
   u    /|  u  /|u    /| u  /|  u   /
```
And Thee, across the harbor, silver paced
```
u    /  |  u /|  /   /|  u  /|  u   /
```
As though the sun took step of thee yet left
```
    \    /|  u  /|u /|u  u|  /   /
```
Some motion ever unspent in thy stride,—
```
   u /|u /|u    /|  u   /|  u   /
```
Implicitly thy freedom staying thee!

Claude McKay

IF WE MUST DIE   Iambic pentameter

u / | u / | / u | u / | u /
If we must die—let it not be like hogs

/   u | u / | u u | u / | u u /
Hunted and penned in an inglorious spot,

u   / | u / | u / | u / | u   /
While round us bark the mad and hungry dogs,

/   u | u   / | u / | u / | u   /
Making their mock at our accursèd lot.

/ u | u   / | u / | u / | u /
If we must die, O let us nobly die,

u / | u   / | u / | u / | u /
So that our precious blood may not be shed

u / | u / | u u / | u   / | u /
In vain; then even the monsters we defy

u   / | u / | u / | u / | u   /
Shall be constrained to honor us though dead!

/ / | u / | u / | u / | u   /
O kinsmen! we must meet the common foe!

u   / | u / | u / | / \ | / \
Though far outnumbered let us show us brave,

u / | u   / | u / | / u | / /
And for their thousand blows deal one death-blow!

/   \ | u / | u / | u / | u /
What though before us lies the open grave?

/   / | u   / | u / | u u / | u u /
Like men we'll face the murderous, cowardly pack,

/   u | u / | / u | u / | u   /
Pressed to the wall, dying, but fighting back!

Jessie Redmon Fauset

RAIN FUGUE   **Trochaic tetrameter**

/ u | / u | / u | / (u)
Slanting, driving, Summer rain

/ u | / u | / u| / (u)
How you wash my heart of pain!

/ u | / u | / u| / (u)
How you make me think of trees,

/ u | / u | / u | / (u)
Ships and gulls and flashing seas!

/ u | / u u | / u | / (u)
In your furious, tearing wind,

/ u| / u | / u | / (u)
Swells a chant that heals my mind;

/ u | / u | / u | / (u)
And your passion high and proud,

/ u | / u | / u| / (u)
Makes me shout and laugh aloud!

/ u | / u | / u | / (u)
Autumn rains that start at dawn,

/ u | / u| / u | / (u)
"Dropping veils of thinnest lawn,"

/ u| / u | / u | / u
Soaking sod between dank grasses,

/ u | / u | / u | / u
Sweeping golden leaves in masses,—

/ u | / u | / u | / (u)
Blotting, blurring out the Past,

/ u | /   u | /   u | / (u)
In a dream you hold me fast;

/   u | /   u | / u | / (u)
Calling, coaxing to forget

/   u | /   u | /   u | / (u)
Things that are, for things not yet.

/ u | /   u | /   u | / (u)
Winter tempest, winter rain,

/   u | /   u | /   u | / (u)
Hurtling down with might and main,

/   u | /   u | / u | /   (u)
You but make me hug my hearth,

/   u | /   u | /   u | /   (u)
Laughing, sheltered from your wrath.

/   u | /   u | /   u | / (u)
Now I woo my dancing fire,

/ u | / u | /   u | / u
Piling, piling drift-wood higher.

/   u | /   u | /   u | / (u)
Books and friends and pictures old,

/   u | /   u | /   u | / (u)
Hearten while you pound and scold!

/ u u | / u | /   u u | /   (u)
Pattering, wistful showers of Spring

/   u | / u | / u | / (u)
Set me to remembering

/   u | /   u | / u | / (u)
Far-off times and lovers too,

```
  /   u  | /    u  | /    u  | / (u)
```
Gentle joys and heart-break rue,—
```
  /  u  u | /  u| /   u| /  (u)
```
Memories I'd as lief forget,
```
   /    u  u|/ u u |/  u| / (u)
```
Were not oblivion sadder yet.
```
  /  u  | /   u  | /   u  | / (u)
```
Ah! you twist my mind with pain,
```
  /  u | /   u   u | / u | / (u)
```
Wistful, whispering April rain!

```
  /   u  | /  u   | /  u| / (u)
```
Summer, Autumn, Winter rain,
```
  /   u  | /  u  | /   u| / (u)
```
How you ease my heart of pain!
```
  /  u  u  | /  u  | /  u  u| /    (u)
```
Whispering, wistful showers of Spring,
```
  /   u| /   u | /  u  | / (u)
```
How I love the hurt you bring!

William Stanley Braithwaite

A SEA-PRAYER **Trochaic trimeter**

```
  /    u| /   u  | / u
```
LORD of wind and water
```
  /    u| /   u | /  (u)
```
Where the ships go down
```
  /    u  | /  u | /  \
```
Reaching to the sunrise,

/ u | / u | / (u)
Lifting like a crown,

/ u | u / | / u   [/ u u | / # | / u]
Out of the deep-hidden [Out of the deep-hidden]

/ u | / u | / (u)
Wells of night and day —

/ u | / \ | / u
Mind the great sea-farers

/ u | / u | / (u)
On the open way.

/ u | / \ | / u
When the last lights darken

/ u | / \ | / (u)
On the far coastline,

/ u | / u | / u
Wave and port and peril

/ \ | / u | / (u)
Sea-Lord — all are thine.

Henry Wadsworth Longfellow

From THE SONG OF HIAWATHA   **Trochaic tetrameter**

/ u | / u | / u | / u
Thus it was that in the North-land

/ u | / u | / u | / u
After that unheard-of coldness,

/ u | / u | / u | / u
That intolerable Winter,

```
  /   u  | /      u  | / u| / u
```
Came the Spring with all its splendor,
```
/  u| /     u  | / u| / u
```
All its birds and all its blossoms,
```
/  u| /  u   u | /    u  | / u
```
All its flowers and leaves and grasses.
```
  /  u | / u | /    u| / u
```
 Sailing on the wind to northward,
```
/  u | /  \  | /       \ | / u
```
Flying in great flocks, like arrows,
```
/       /  | / u | /   \    | / u
```
Like huge arrows shot through heaven,
```
/     u | /    u | / u| / u
```
Passed the swan, the Mahnahbezee,
```
/    u  | / u| / u| /    \
```
Speaking almost as a man speaks;
```
/   u| /    /  | / u | / u
```
And in long lines waving, bending
```
/   u| /    \  | /       u| / u
```
Like a bow-string snapped asunder,
```
/    u  | /  u  | /  u| / u
```
Came the white goose, Waw-be-wawa;
```
/  u| /   u| / u | / u
```
And in pairs, or singly flying,
```
/      u | /    u | / u u | / u
```
Mahng the loon, with clangorous pinions,
```
u    / | / u  | u   /  | /  u
```
The blue heron, the Shuh-shuh-gah,
```
/  u | /     u | /  u| / u
```
And the grouse, the Mushkodasa.

/ u | / u | / u | / u
In the thickets and the meadows

/   u | / \ | / u | / u
Piped the bluebird, the Owaissa,

/ u | / u | / u | / u
On the summit of the lodges

/ u | / u | u u | / u
Sang the robin, the Opechee,

/ u | / u | / u | / u
In the covert of the pine-trees

/   u | / u | u u | / u
Cooed the pigeon, the Omemee;

William Blake

THE TYGER   **Trochaic tetrameter**

/ u | / u | / u | / (u)
Tyger Tyger, burning bright,

/ u | / u | / u | / (u)
In the forests of the night;

/   u | / u | /   u | / (u)
What immortal hand or eye,

(u)   \   / | / u | / u | / (u)
Could frame thy fearful symmetry?

/ u | / u | /   u | / (u)
In what distant deeps or skies.

/   u | / u | / u | / (u)
Burnt the fire of thine eyes?

/ u | /   u | / u|/ (u)
On what wings dare he aspire?
/   u | /   / | /   u | / u
What the hand, dare seize the fire?

/   u | / u | / u | / (u)
And what shoulder, & what art,
 u   / | u /| u /| u   /
Could twist the sinews of thy heart?
u   / | u   / | u / | u /
And when thy heart began to beat.
 /   \ | /   u | /   \ | /   (u)
What dread hand? & what dread feet?

/   u | /   u | /   u| / (u)
What the hammer? what the chain,
/ u | / u | / u | / (u)
In what furnace was thy brain?
/   u | / u | /   \ | / (u)
What the anvil? what dread grasp.
/   u | / u | / u | /   (u)
Dare its deadly terrors clasp?

 /   u | /   u | /   u | / (u)
When the stars threw down their spears
 u   /| u   /| u / | u   /
And water'd heaven with their tears:
/ u | /   u | /   u| / (u)
Did he smile his work to see?

/ u | u / | u / | \ /
Did he who made the Lamb make thee?

/ u | / u | / u | / (u)
Tyger Tyger, burning bright,
/ u | / u | / u | / (u)
In the forests of the night;
/   u | / u | /   u | / (u)
What immortal hand or eye,
/   / | u / | u / | u /
Dare frame thy fearful symmetry?

Autumn Newman

SHEDDING SKIN   Dactylic tetrameter and trimeter

/ u u | / u \ | / u   u | / u (u)
This is a thunderclap splitting the silence.
/ u u | / u   u | /   (u u)
This is the lightning bolt thrown.

/ u u | / \ | / u   u | / u u
This is a pain like you could not give to me.
/ u u | / u u | / (u u)
This is the hollow in stone.

/ u u | / u u | / u u | / u (u)
This is too seismic, unsteady and sudden.
/ u u | / u u | / (u u)
This is the cracking of bone.

/ u u | /   u u | /   u u | / u (u)
This is a breath that is drenched in the sacred.
/   u   u | / u | / (u u)
This is the rain alone.

/   u u | / u u | / u   \ | / u (u)
This is my body, a flower burst open.
/   u u | / u   \ | /   (u u)
This is the color I've grown.

Paul Laurence Dunbar

THE PARADOX   Dactylic trimeter

/ u u | / u   u | / u (u)
I am the mother of sorrows,
  / u   u | / u u | / (u u)
  I am the ender of grief;
/ u u | / u   u | / u (u)
I am the bud and the blossom,
  / u   u | / \ u | / (u u)
  I am the late-falling leaf.

/ u u | /   u u | / u (u)
I am thy priest and thy poet,
  / u u | /   u u | / (u u)
  I am thy serf and thy king;
/ \ u | / u u | / \ (u)
I cure the tears of the heartsick,
  /   u \ | / u   u | / (u u)
  When I come near they shall sing.

```
   /    u  u | /    u u | /  u (u)
```
White are my hands as the snowdrop;
```
     /     u  u| /  u u | / (u u)
```
  Swart are my fingers as clay;
```
  /    u u |/    u u | /  u (u)
```
Dark is my frown as the midnight,
```
    /   u  u | /     u u | / (u u)
```
  Fair is my brow as the day.

```
 / u   u  | /   u   u | /  u (u)
```
Battle and war are my minions,
```
   /  u  u | /   u u | / (u u)
```
  Doing my will as divine;
```
/ u   u | /   u  u | /  u (u)
```
I am the calmer of passions,
```
   /      u u| /    u  u| /  (u u)
```
  Peace is a nursling of mine.

```
  /    u  u | / u  u | /   u (u)
```
Speak to me gently or curse me,
```
    /   u  u| /   u   u | / (u u)
```
  Seek me or fly from my sight;
```
/ u   u  | /    u u | /  u (u)
```
I am thy fool in the morning,
```
    /   u  u | /    u u | / (u u)
```
  Thou art my slave in the night.

```
  /    u  u | /  u  u| /  u (u)
```
Down to the grave will I take thee,

/ u u| / u u| / (u u)
Out from the noise of the strife;
/ / / | / u u | / u (u)
Then shalt thou see me and know me—
/   u   u |/ u   u | / (u u)
Death, then, no longer, but life.

/ u / | / u u | / u (u)
Then shalt thou sing at my coming,
/ u u |/ u u | / (u u)
Kiss me with passionate breath,
/ u u | / u u | / u (u)
Clasp me and smile to have thought me
/   u u | / \ u| / (u u)
Aught save the foeman of Death.

/ u u | / u   \ | / u (u)
Come to me, brother, when weary,
/   u u | / u / | / (u u)
Come when thy lonely heart swells;
/ \   u | / u   u | / u (u)
I'll guide thy footsteps and lead thee
/   u u | / \ u | / (u u)
Down where the Dream Woman dwells.

Elizabeth Akers Allen

ROCK ME TO SLEEP   **Dactylic tetrameter**

/ u u | / u u | / u u | / (u u)
Backward, turn backward, O Time, in your flight,
/   u u | / u \ | / u u | / (u u)
Make me a child again just for tonight!
/ u u | / u u | / u u | / (u u)
Mother, come back from the echoless shore,
/ u u | / u u | / u u | / (u u)
Take me again to your heart as of yore;
/   u u | / \ u | / u u | / (u u)
Kiss from my forehead the furrows of care,
/   u / | / u / | / u u | / (u u)
Smooth the few silver threads out of my hair;
/ u u | / u \ | / u   \ | /   (u u)
Over my slumbers your loving watch keep;—
/   u u | / \ u | / u u | / (u u)
Rock me to sleep, mother, – rock me to sleep!

/ u u | / u   / | / u u | / (u u)
Backward, flow backward, O tide of the years!
/ u u | / u u | / u u | / (u u)
I am so weary of toil and of tears,—
/   u u | / u u | /   u u | / (u u)
Toil without recompense, tears all in vain,—
/ u u | / u u | / u u | / (u u)
Take them, and give me my childhood again!
/ u   u | / u u | / u u | / (u u)
I have grown weary of dust and decay,—

```
/  u  u| /  u  u | /    \    u |/   (u u)
```
Weary of flinging my soul-wealth away
```
/  u  u| /  u  u | /  u  u| /   (u u)
```
Weary of sowing for others to reap;—
```
/    u u|  /   \  u  | /   u u| /   (u u)
```
Rock me to sleep, mother – rock me to sleep!

```
/    u u | / u  u| /    u u | /   (u u)
```
Tired of the hollow, the base, the untrue,
```
/   u  / | / u   u | /    u  u | /   (u u)
```
Mother, O mother, my heart calls for you!
```
/  u u| /  u  u | / u   \  | /     (u u)
```
Many a summer the grass has grown green,
```
/   u    u | / u   u |/ u u | /   (u u)
```
Blossomed and faded, our faces between:
```
/   u    /   | / u   u  | / u u  | /   (u u)
```
Yet, with strong yearning and passionate pain,
```
/    u u| /   u   u  | /  u  u| /   (u u)
```
Long I tonight for your presence again.
```
/     u   u | / u  u| /  u  u| /   (u u)
```
Come from the silence so long and so deep;—
```
/    u u| /   \  u  | /   u u| /   (u u)
```
Rock me to sleep, mother, – rock me to sleep!

```
/ u  u | /    u u| /   u  u | /   (u u)
```
Over my heart, in the days that are flown,
```
/   /   \  | / u   /  |/ u  u | /   (u u)
```
No love like mother-love ever has shone;
```
/  \ u  | /  u   u|/   u  u | /   (u u)
```
No other worship abides and endures,—

How to Scan a Poem

/   u u|/ u   u | / u u | /   (u u)
Faithful, unselfish, and patient like yours:
/   \ u| / u /|/   u u | /   (u u)
None like a mother can charm away pain
/   u \ | / u   u|/   / u| /   (u u)
From the sick soul and the world-weary brain.
/   u   / |/ \ \ |/ u / | /   (u u)
Slumber's soft calms o'er my heavy lids creep;—
/   u u| /   \ u | /   u u |/   (u u)
Rock me to sleep, mother, – rock me to sleep!

/   \ u | /   \ u| / u u |/   (u u)
Come, let your brown hair, just lighted with gold,
/ u \ | / u   u|/ u u| /   (u u)
Fall on your shoulders again as of old;
/ u / | / u \| /   \ u | /   (u u)
Let it drop over my forehead tonight,
/ u   u | /   / u|/ u u | /   (u u)
Shading my faint eyes away from the light;
u \ u|/ u u |/ u   u | /   (u u)
For with its sunny-edged shadows once more
/ u u |/   u / | / u u| /   (u u)
Haply will throng the sweet visions of yore;
/ u u |/ u u| /   / u | /   (u u)
Lovingly, softly, its bright billows sweep;—
/   u u| / \ u | / u u|/   (u u)
Rock me to sleep, mother, – rock me to sleep!

/ u u |/ u u|/ u u |/   (u u)
Mother, dear mother, the years have been long

/ u u | / u u | /u u | / (u u)
Since I last listened your lullaby song:

/ u u |/ u u | / u / | / (u u)
Sing, then, and unto my soul it shall seem

/ u u | / u u |/ u u | / (u u)
Womanhood's years have been only a dream.

/ u u | / u u| / u u | / (u u)
Clasped to your heart in a loving embrace,

u \ / |/ u u | / u u | / (u u)
With your light lashes just sweeping my face,

/ u u|/ u u| / u u| / (u u)
Never hereafter to wake or to weep;—

/ u u| / \ u | / u u| / (u u)
Rock me to sleep, mother, – rock me to sleep!

Annie Finch

ENCOUNTER   Dactylic pentameter

/ u u | / u \ | / u u | / u| / (uu)
Then, in the bus where strange eyes are believed to burn

/ u u|/ u u | / u | / u | / (uu)
down into separate depths, ours mingled, lured

/ u u| / u | / u u | / u| / (uu)
out of the crowd like wings—and as fast, as blurred.

(u) / \ u|/ u u|/ u u | / u| / (u)
We brushed past the others and rose. We had flight to learn,

/ u u| / u u|/ u u | / u u | / (u)
single as wings, til we saw we could merge with a turn,

How to Scan a Poem

/ u u | / u u| / \ u | /   u | / (u)
arching our gazing together. We formed one bird,

/ u   u|/ u | / u u| / u u | / (u)
focused, attentive. Flying in silence, we heard

(u) / u u | / u u| / u   u |/   u u | / (uu)
the air past our feathers, the wind through our feet, and the churn

(u) /   u u | /(#)| / u   u| / u \ | / (uu)
of wheels in the dark. Now we have settled. We move

/ u   \ | / u | / u | / u | / (uu)
calmly, two balanced creatures. Opened child,

/ u u|/ u| / u u | /   u | / (uu)
woman or man, companion with whom I've flown

  /   u u| / u u | / u | / u | / (uu)
through this remembering, lost, incarnate love,

/ u u|/ u u | /   / | u \ | / (uu)
turning away, we will land, growing more wild

(u) / u| / u   u| / u u| /   u | / (uu)
with solitude, more alone, than we could have known.

Thomas Hardy

THE VOICE   **Dactylic tetrameter**

/ u u | /   u u |/ u u| / u u
Woman much missed, how you call to me, call to me,

/ u   u | / u u | / u u | / (u u)
Saying that now you are not as you were

/   u u | /   u u |/ u u |/ u u
When you had changed from the one who was all to me,

116

/ u u| /   u   u| /   u | / (u u)
But as at first, when our day was fair.

/   u u| /   u u| /   \ u | /   u   u
Can it be you that I hear? Let me view you, then,

/   u u | / u / |/   u u| / (u u)
Standing as when I drew near to the town

/   u   \ | / u \| /   u\| /   u   u
Where you would wait for me: yes, as I knew you then,

/ u u u u|/ u u|/   \ | /   (u)
Even to the original air-blue gown!

/ u u|/ u u | /   u u| / u   u
Or is it only the breeze, in its listlessness

/ u u   u | / u / | /   u / |/ (u u)
Traveling across the wet mead to me here,

/   u u | / u u| /   u u | / u u
You being ever dissolved to wan wistlessness,

/   u u   u|/ / u | /   (u u)
Heard no more again far or near?

   / u| / u u | / u (u)
   Thus I; faltering forward,

   /   u| /   u | / u (u)
   Leaves around me falling,

/ u u | / u   u| /   u | / u (u)
Wind oozing thin through the thorn from norward,

   / u| / u | / u (u)
   And the woman calling.

Annie Finch

MY SISTER WHO KEPT HER ABORTION A SECRET   Amphibrachic tetrameter

```
u  / u |  u  / u | u  / u | u  / u
```
My sister — the daring, the rider, the dancer —
```
u     / u | u  / u | u  /  u | u  / u
```
Whose silence put her in the path of this danger —
```
u  / u | u  /  u | u  /  u | u  / u
```
Is breaking the heart of my question or answer
```
u  / u | u  /    u | u  /   u | u  / u
```
Again, as she moves off to death, like a stranger.

```
u    /   u | u  /  u | u  / u | u  /   u
```
She's spun herself on. And the poisons that filled her?
```
u  / u | u  / u | u    /  \ | u  / u
```
The secret that fed her? Those heart-heavy chances
```
u  / u  | u  / u | u / u | u   /    u
```
Her life stole and killed until, finally, they spilled her
```
(u) /  u   | u  / u | u   /   u | u  / u
```
   Out through the universe? Those were her dances.

```
u  / u | u  / u |  u  / u | u  /   u
```
No mother has held her — No village will mourn her —
```
u /u | u  /   u  |  /   /  u | u  / u
```
No ritual frames her —Come, help me reclaim her —
```
u  / u | u   /  u | u / u | u  /   u
```
Her body won't bear her again — nor be borne. Her
```
u  /  u | u  / u | u   /  / | / / u
```
true name is no secret — and — we will not blame her.

```
u   / u | u   / u  | u   / u | u   / u
```
My sister, the daring, the rider, the dancer
```
u     /   u | u    /    u | u   / u | u   / u
```
Who steps out, who stepped in the path of the danger.

Samuel Woodworth

THE OLD OAKEN BUCKET   **Amphibrachic tetrameter**

```
u    /  u|  \   /    u | u   /    u | u    /   \
```
How dear to this heart are the scenes of my childhood,
```
u     /   u | u / u | u   /   u | u   /  (u)
```
When fond recollection presents them to view!
```
u   /  u  | u   /  u | u   /   \ | u   /  u
```
The orchard, the meadow, the deep-tangled wild-wood,
```
u   /  u|   /    /    u  | u   / u | u   /   (u)
```
And every loved spot that my infancy knew!
```
u    /     /  | u   /    u | u   /  u |  /   / u
```
The wide-spreading pond, and the mill that stood by it,
```
u    /     u | u   /    u   | u   / u | u   /  (u)
```
The bridge, and the rock where the cataract fell,
```
u   /  u | u   / u | u   / u |  \    /  u
```
The cot of my father, the dairy-house nigh it,
```
u    /   u|   /   / u  | u   /   u | u  /  (u)
```
And e'en the rude bucket that hung in the well—
```
u    /   / | u   /   u  | u   / u |  \    /  u
```
The old oaken bucket, the iron-bound bucket,
```
u    /   \ |  u    /   u | u     /   u | u   /  (u)
```
The moss-covered bucket which hung in the well.
```
u    /    \ | u    /   u | u   /    u | u   /  u
```
That moss-covered bucket I hailed as a treasure,

How to Scan a Poem

   u   / u | u /   u | u /   u | u / (u)
For often at noon, when return'd from the field,

  u   /   u|u /   u| u / u| u /   u
I found it the source of an exquisite pleasure,

  u   / u |u /   u | u / u | u   /   (u)
The purest and sweetest that nature can yield.

  u   / u |u /   u|u   /   \| u   /   u
How ardent I seized it, with hands that were glowing,

  u   /   u|u   /   \| u   / u |u / (u)
And quick to the white pebbled bottom it fell

  u   /   u | u /   u | u /   \|u / u
Then soon, with the emblem of truth o'erflowing,

  u   / u | u   / u |u / u | u   / (u)
And dripping with coolness, it rose from the well.

  u   /   u |u /   \|u /   u|u / u
How sweet from the green, mossy brim to receive it,

  u   /   u|u /   u|u   /   u|u / (u)
As, poised on the curb, it inclined to my lips!

(u) u /   \| u / u | u   /   u | u /   u
Not a full blushing goblet could tempt me to leave it,

  u   /   u |u / u| u /u|u / (u)
Tho' filled with the nectar that Jupiter sips.

  u   /   / | u /   u |u   /   /|u /u
And now, far removed from the loved habitation,

  u   /   u|u /   u |u / u|u   /   (u)
The tear of regret will intrusively swell,

 u / u | u / u|u / u | u / u
As fancy reverts to my father's plantation,

  u   /   \ |u / u | u   / u|u / (u)
And sighs for the bucket that hung in the well.

Austin Allen

THERE ONCE WAS   **Amphibrachic trimeter and dimeter**

  u / u | u   / u | u / (u)
A tango that's also a waltz—
  u / u | u / u| u / (u)
A rhythm that awkwardly halts,
   u /   u| u / u
But sways a few hearers
  u / \ | u   / u
In old barroom mirrors
  u / \|u /   u | u / (u)
That say every form has its faults.

*

    u   /   u |u / u | u / u
There once was a gentleman listed
u   /   u | u   / u|u / u
Among those who never existed.
u   /   u | u / u
His colleagues politely
u / u | u   / u
Reminded him nightly—
u   /   u|u   /   u | u / u
He woke in a sweat and persisted.

u /   u |u / u| u / (u)
I leaf through a yellowing tome.
  u   /   u |u / u| u / (u)
They must have retired the gloam
u   /   \| u / (u)
In, what, 1910?

(u) / u | # / u | u / (u)
  Only twilight since then.

u / u | u / u | u   /   (u)
I'm homesick for when I missed home.

  u   /   u | u /   u | u / u (u)
There once was a State Representative

 u   /   u | u /   u | u / u (u)
Who feared that her base would resent it if

u / u | u / (u)
She didn't erase

(u) u / u | u / (u)
Both herself and her base.

u / u | u / u | u / u (u)
Till autumn, the plan remained tentative.

\ /   u | u / u | u / (u)
I speak out. I feel that I must.

\ / u | u   /   u | u / (u)
I hear my own spiel with disgust.

\ / \ | u / (u)
I see others make

(u) u / u | u / (u)
My egregious mistake.

\ / u | u / u | u / (u)
I speak out. I feel that I must.

u / u | u / u | u / \
The gesture, the comment, the eyeroll—

u / u | u / u | \ / u
The germ of a fury gone viral—

u / \ | u / (u)
The long, glowing dream

(u) u /   u | u /   (u)
Of a scroll or a stream

 u   /   u | /   / u | u / u
That seems to twist into a spiral . . .

 u   / u | u   /   u | u / u
The ocelot gazed like a tourist.

 u   / u | u / u | u   / u
No monkeys or parakeets chorused.

 u   / u | u   /   (u)
Fresh radio beats

(u) / u | # / u| u   /   (u)
   Floated over the streets

(u) u   /   u | u   /   u | u / u
Of the precinct that once was a forest.

 u   /   u | u / u | u / (u)
The news is the usual crap—

u / u | \   /   u | u / (u)
I sigh and lie down for a nap.

 u   / u | u   /   (u)
Your body and eyes

(u) u / u | u   / /
Repossess me ... I rise.

 u   /   u | u /   u | u   / (u)
A town's disappeared from the map.

  u   /   u | u   /   u | u \ (u)
Come back while the woods are still wild,

  u   /   u | \   /   u | u / (u)
Come back without mortgage or child,

 u   / u | u   /   (u)
Come riding my way

(u)   u   /   u | u   /   (u)
When the climate in May

 u   /   u | u   /   \ | u   /   (u)
Agrees, for one night, to be mild.

 u   /   u | u /   u | u /   (u)
There once was a time and a place

 \   /   u | u   /   u | u /   (u)
Shaved down to the ghost of a trace

(u) u   /   u | u   /   (u)
Of a scholarly laugh

(u) u   /   u | u   /   (u)
In the last paragraph

(u) u   /   u | u   /   u | u /   (u)
Of a note on an ode to a vase.

 u   /   u | u   /   u | u   /   u
I'm losing the thread of my thesis.

 u   /   u | u   /   u | u   /   u
I once said out loud to my niece's

 u / u | \   /   u
Beloved stuffed penguin,

 u   /   u | u   /   u
Whose smile is so sanguine:

   u   /   \ | u   /   u | u   /   u
"Your whole fucking pole is in pieces."

 u   /   u | u   /   u | u   /   (u)
They're fighting a war overseas;

 u   /   \ | u   /   u | u   /   (u)
We can't seem to locate our keys;

```
u   /  u | u  /  u
```
A column's been slaughtered;

```
 u   /   u | u / u
```
Our plants are unwatered;

```
 u   /   \   | u / u | u /  (u)
```
Our windshield's beginning to freeze.


```
 u     /   u  | u / u | u / u
```
There once was a girl at the border.

```
u  / u |   /   u  | u / u
```
Her papers were squarely in order.

```
u   / u | u  /   (u)
```
The quieter guard

```
(u) / u  |# / u |  u   /   (u)
```
   Started staring too hard.

```
u    /   u | u / u | u / u
```
There once was a girl at the border.


```
  u    /    u | u / u | u /  (u)
```
There once was a noble intent,

```
 u  /   /   | u / u | u  /  (u)
```
A clean breeze, a stabilized rent,

```
u   / u | u  /  u
```
The passenger pigeon,

```
u   / u | u   /  u
```
My grandmother's kitchen,

```
u / u| u / u | u   /   (u)
```
Aretha, Pangaea, your scent . . .


```
 u     /    u | u / u | u / u
```
There once was a civilization

```
u     /   u |u  /  u | u / u
```
Whose peak was of modest duration.

```
u  / u|   \    /   (u)
```
An upside-down spire

```
 /  /  u |u  /  (u)
```
Juts out of the mire,

```
u     /   u |u /  u |u / u
```
Which bubbles a long exhalation.

Anna Akhmatova

LOT'S WIFE   Amphibrachic tetrameter

"But his wife looked back from behind him, and she became a pillar of salt."
— Genesis 19:25-26

```
u   /   u  | /  / u  | u    /    \|u  /   (u)
```
The righteous man followed where God's angel guide

```
u    /    u    |\    /   u    |u / u  |u   /    (u)
```
shone on through black mountains, imposing and bright—

```
u   /   \ | u  /    /   |u   /   u| u / (u)
```
but pain tore his wife's breast. It turned her aside

```
u   /     \ | u /    u |u  /   u |u  /   (u)
```
and said, "Look again! There is time for one sight

```
u  / u |  u  / u  | / /    u |u  /  (u)
```
Of towers, and Sodom's red halls, and the place

```
(u)    \   /   u |u  /   u  |u  /  u| u   /  (u)
```
Where you sang in the courtyard or wove on your loom

```
u   /   u | u  / u  |  u    u  /    u |u  /
```
By windows now empty—where you knew the embrace

```
u  /   u | u  /   u |  u   /     / | u  /  (u)
```
Of love with your husband—where birth filled the room—."

```
  u   /     u | u  /   u | u  /  u | u  /  (u)
```
She looked. And the sight was more bitter than pain.
```
  u  /  \| u   /   \| u  /   \| u   /   (u)
```
It shut up her eyes so she saw nothing more;
```
  u  /   u   | u  / # | u  /   \   | u  /  (u)
```
She shimmered to salt; her feet moved in vain,
```
   /    / u | u  /   \| u  /    \ | # /   u
```
Deep rooted at last in the place she died for.

```
  u   /    u | /  /    u | u  /   u | u  /  (u)
```
Who weeps for her now? Who can care for the fate
```
  u  /   \  | u   /   u| \    /  \| u   /   (u)
```
Of someone like that—a mere unhappy wife?
```
   /   /    u | u  /   u  | u / u | u  /   (u)
```
My heart will remember. I carry the weight
```
  u  /   / |  /     /     \   | u  /   \ | \   /  (u)
```
Of one who looked back, though it cost her her life.

Robert Frost

FOR ONCE, THEN, SOMETHING　　**Hendecasyllabic**

```
 /  u | /     u  u | /  u | /    u | /    \
```
Others taunt me with having knelt at well-curbs
```
 /  u  | /     u  u| /   / | /  u| /  u
```
Always wrong to the light, so never seeing
```
 /  u | /    u  u | /   \ | /    u  | /  u
```
Deeper down in the well than where the water
```
 /    \ | /    u  u| /  u| /   u | /  u
```
Gives me back in a shining surface picture

127

/ \ | / u u | / u | / u | / /
Me myself in the summer heaven godlike

/ u | / u u | / u | / u | / \
Looking out of a wreath of fern and cloud puffs.

/ / | / u u | / u | / u | / u
Once, when trying with chin against a well-curb,

/ u | / u u | / u | / u | / u
I discerned, as I thought, beyond the picture,

/ u | / u u | / u | / u | / u
Through the picture, a something white, uncertain,

/ u | / u u | / u | / \ | / u
Something more of the depths—and then I lost it.

/ u | / u u | / u | / / | / u
Water came to rebuke the too clear water.

/ / | / u u | / u | / u | / u
One drop fell from a fern, and lo, a ripple

/ u | / u u | / / | / u | / u
Shook whatever it was lay there at bottom,

/ u | / u u | / \ | / u | / u
Blurred it, blotted it out. What was that whiteness?

/ u | / u u | / u | / \ | / u
Truth? A pebble of quartz? For once, then, something.

Patricia Smith

THE REEMERGENCE OF THE NOOSE   **Hendecasyllabic**

/ u | / u u | / u | / u | / u
Some lamp sputters its dusky light across a

/ u | / u u | / u | / u | / u
desk. Some hand, in a fever, works the fraying

```
 /     \  | /  u   u| / u  | / u  | / u
```
brown hemp, twisting and knifing, weaving, tugging
```
 /      u | / u u | / u | / u | / u
```
tight this bellowing circle. Randy Travis
```
 /      /  | / u u| / u | /     u | / u
```
sings, moans, radios steamy twangs and hiccups,
```
 /     \  | /  u   u| / u | \ u | / u
```
blue notes backing the ritual of drooping
```
 /      /  | /  u u| / u  | / u| / u
```
loop. Sweat drips in an awkward hallelujah.
```
 /     \ | /     u  u| / u| / u | / u
```
God glares down, but the artist doesn't waver—
```
 /      / | /  u   u | /   u  | / u| / u
```
wrists click rhythm, and rope becomes a path to
```
 /     \  | /  u   u| /   u | /   u| / u
```
what makes saviors; the loop bemoans its need to
```
 /       u| /  u   u  u| /   u| / u | / (u)
```
squeeze, its craving for the ghost of Negro neck.

John Masefield

SEA FEVER **Dipodic iambic heptameter**

```
 u  // | u  /  | u u // | u / || u u  // | u  / | u  u //
```
I must go down to the seas again, to the lonely sea and the sky,
```
 u  // | u / | u u  // | # / || / u // | u  /  | u //
```
And all I ask is a tall ship and a star to steer her by,
```
 u   u  //  | # / | u u  //  | # / || u u  //  | u  / | # / (u)
```
And the wheel's kick and the wind's song and the white sail's shaking,

u u // |#/ |u u   // |#/ ‖ u u // |#/ | # // (u)
And a grey mist on the sea's face, and a grey dawn breaking.

u // | u   / | u u // | u /‖ u u   // | u u / | u //
I must go down to the seas again, for the call of the running tide
u u // |#/ | u u // |#/‖ u // | \   / | u //
Is a wild call and a clear call that may not be denied;
  u   // | u / | u u // | u / ‖ u   u   // | \   // (u)
And all I ask is a windy day with the white clouds flying,
  u   u   // |#/ | u u   // |#/   ‖ u u // | \   // (u)
And the flung spray and the blown spume, and the sea-gulls crying.
u // | u   / | u u // | u /‖ u u // | u   / | u //

I must go down to the seas again, to the vagrant gypsy life,
  u   u   // |#/ | u u   // |#/ ‖ u u   // | u u / | u //
To the gull's way and the whale's way, where the wind's like a whetted knife;
  u   // | u / | u u // | u / ‖ u u // | u   / | u // (u)
And all I ask is a merry yarn from a laughing fellow-rover,
 u   // | u   / | u u // |#/ ‖ u u   // | #/ | #// (u)
And quiet sleep and a sweet dream when the long trick's over.

Edgar Allan Poe

from THE RAVEN   Dipodic trochaic octameter

//   u | / u | //   u | / u | // u | / u | //   u | / u
Once upon a midnight dreary, while I pondered weak and weary,
// u | / u u | //   u | / u u | // u | / u | // u | / (u)
Over many a quaint and curious volume of forgotten lore,
//   u | / u | // u | / u | // u | / u | // u | / u
While I nodded, nearly napping, suddenly there came a tapping,

// u| /   u|// u| / u |// u |/ u| // u | / (u)
As of some one gently rapping, rapping at my chamber door.
 /   u |// u|/ u| // u ||// u|/ u | // u | / (u)
`'Tis some visitor,' I muttered, `tapping at my chamber door -
// u| /   u | // u | / (u)
Only this, and nothing more.'

// u|/ u|// u|/ u |// u |/ u| //   u | / u
Ah, distinctly I remember it was in the bleak December,
//   u | / u |// u|/ u| //   u | / u|// u | / (u)
And each separate dying ember wrought its ghost upon the floor.
//u|/ u| //   u |/ u || // u|/ u| // u |/ u
Eagerly I wished the morrow; - vainly I had sought to borrow
//   u| //   u | / u| / u || // u | / u | // u | / (u)
From my books surcease of sorrow - sorrow for the lost Lenore -
/   u| //   u|// u u| / u | /   u | // u | / u | // (u)
For the rare and radiant maiden whom the angels name Lenore -
//   u| /   u| // u| / (u)
Nameless here for evermore.

//   u | // u| / u | / u | // u| / u | // u | / u
And the silken sad uncertain rustling of each purple curtain
//   u || / u | / u |// u | // u| / u| // u | / (u)
Thrilled me - filled me with fantastic terrors never felt before;
/   u| // u|/ u | // u | / u | // u | /   u |// u
So that now, to still the beating of my heart, I stood repeating
/   u |// u|/ u|// u || // u | / u | / u | // (u)
`'Tis some visitor entreating entrance at my chamber door -
/   u | // u| / u| // u| // u| / u | // u | / (u)
Some late visitor entreating entrance at my chamber door; -

/ u | // u | / u | // (u)
This it is, and nothing more,'

/ u | / u | // u | // u | // u | / u | / u | // u
Presently my soul grew stronger; hesitating then no longer,
// u | / u | // u || / u | / u | // u | / u | // (u)
'Sir,' said I, 'or Madam, truly your forgiveness I implore;
/ u | // u | / u | // u || / u | // u | / u | // u
But the fact is I was napping, and so gently you came rapping,
/ u | // u | / u | / u || // u | / u | // u | // (u)
And so faintly you came tapping, tapping at my chamber door,
/ u | / u | // u | // u || / u | // u | / u | // (u)
That I scarce was sure I heard you' - here I opened wide the door; -
// u | / u | // u | / (u)
Darkness there, and nothing more.

/ u | / u | // u | / u | // u | / u | // u | // u
Deep into that darkness peering, long I stood there wondering, fearing,
// u || / u | // u | // u | / u | // u | / u | / (u)
Doubting, dreaming dreams no mortal ever dared to dream before;
/ u | // u | / u | // u | / u | // u | / u | // u
But the silence was unbroken, and the darkness gave no token,
/ u | // u | / u | // u | / u | // u | / u | // (u)
And the only word there spoken was the whispered word, 'Lenore!'
// u | / u | / u | // u | / u | // u | / u | // (u)
This I whispered, and an echo murmured back the word, 'Lenore!'
// u | / u | // u | / (u)
Merely this and nothing more.

Afterword

BEYOND SCANSION: A FEW NOTES TO GO BEYOND SCANSION

These brief notes suggest a few of the deeper, further directions in which scansion can take us…

Scanning poems in the wild

Eventually, you will need to apply the three-step method to raw poems that your ear may recognize as being in meter, but about whose meter you know nothing. It should be OK. As with any art, experience and familiarity will make things infinitely easier to understand, and there are enough examples of each meter in this book to give you a feel for the meter so that, somewhere in the process of applying the three-step method to an unfamiliar poem, it will likely dawn on you, perhaps through a physical sensation, what the meter is. If that doesn't happen, compare the poem to meters in this book, including accentuals. If it still isn't clear, it may be that the poem is not in a meter after all. (As a last resort, I am always happy to answer a meter question, so in a pinch, you are invited to contact me through my website if you are stumped!)

A way to give up a scansion you love

Like writing a poem, scanning a poem can be a process of revision. And revision often means discarding things we love (Theodore Roethke called this "murdering your darlings"). I hate to give up things I love, so I usually find ways to satisfy, on some level, my desire to keep them. In scansion, I sometimes save my darlings with the idea of "counterpoint."

Say you are scanning a dactylic poem and you are excited by the subtle anapestic pattern in a certain passage, but you know it would not be helpful to mark this as part of the scansion since the base meter of the poem is dactylic. When we feel a meter strongly but it doesn't fit into the larger metrical pattern of the poem, it is helpful to acknowledge its existence as a subterranean rhythmic stream. This might involve meditating on how it alters the meaning of the poem, notating it in the margin, writing an analysis of the role it plays in the poem (I have written many such analyses, particularly in my book *The Ghost of Meter*), or simply noticing it fully before letting it go. While rhythmical counterpointing may not show up in scansion, it adds contrast and texture and depth and suspense to a poem's meter.

How different lines in the exact same metrical pattern can sound so different

It's amazing how many radically different lines there can be in the exact same meter. How do poets do it? How can they vary the lines so much? Here are the four ways I have observed so far:

> Metrical variations/substitutions
>
> Enjambment from previous or following lines.
>
> Syntax and phrasing

Word rhythm—for example, the presence of a dactylic word will change the rhythm of an iambic line even though if it doesn't change the meter at all.
Word music—assonance, alliteration, and other resonances that play words off each other.

Scansion & Subjectvity: the 80/20 Rule

(Excerpted from *A Poet's Craft/A Poet's Ear* (the sections on meter are the same in both books)

When people first learn how to scan, sometimes they are dismayed to discover the subjective component of meter and scansion. Two people in a group may disagree, for example, on whether a certain syllable in a poem should be stressed or not. Maybe one person has a different pronunciation of the word based on a regional dialect, or a different emotional interpretation of the line. It is not uncommon to feel frustrated at such moments, and perhaps even to be tempted to give up the entire effort. After all, prosody is sometimes dubbed a "science," and if you are going to go to all the trouble to learn it, shouldn't there be a guarantee of solid answers? If there's no clear answer to the simple question, "is this syllable stressed or not?," then maybe there aren't any clear answers. Maybe the whole business of scanning a poem is subjective, and then who's to say that the line is iambic? Why not just call it dactylic? Who could stop me if I said that's how I hear it?

If you are having such thoughts, it may help to remember the 80/20 rule. As a rule, a group of people hearing a given poem will all agree on at least 80% of its scansion—and the proportion is usually higher. The area for disagreement will be 20% or fewer of the syllables in the poem. Furthermore, even in those cases, it's likely the disagreement won't affect the overall scansion of the poem, but only the foot in question. For example, people who hear "fire" pronounced with two syllables will hear the second foot as an anapest in the line, "I fire the smoke and let the heat resound," while people who hear "fire" pronounced with one syllable will hear that foot as an iamb. But whether the second foot is an iamb or an anapest, both groups can still agree that the line is iambic pentameter. Or, in this line by Charles Martin, "Tired of earth, they dwindled on their hill," some will hear "tired" as one syllable and the first line as a headless iambic pentameter; others will hear the first foot as a trochee. But either way, the rest of the line is not affected.

The 80/20 rule assumes a shared basic level of knowledge about meter. You may occasionally encounter people who are so unfamiliar with a certain meter that they are physically unable to hear it; because of the long-reigning dominance of iambic meter in poetry, this sometimes happens with noniambic meters. As with any field of which someone is truly ignorant, in that case discussion may not be possible since even the 80% may not be shared. But in general, you can rest assured that the 20% or less of scansion that is subjective, while it allows for individual variations in linguistic background, speech patterns, personality, mood, and interpretation of the poem, does not make it necessary to throw the validity of the shared, objective 80% of scansion into question, nor to forgo the innumerable benefits of scansion.

Deep scansion

This idea is defined in the definitions page. I won't say more about it here except to say that its possibilities are profound and endless.

Scanning as a way of life

Scanning can put you in touch with the rhythmic language that's already part of you. If you are moved in this way, here are some thoughts to take it further:

Invite bits of language from previous parts of your life to return. It could be a song you knew when you were little, or something someone said to you once, or a name from long ago. Then, notice bits of rhythm that compels you today: a phrase that stays in your mind, or the rhythms of song lyrics. When people speak to you, notice the rhythms of what they say

Once you have some pieces of language, listen for rhythms. Speak them aloud a few times, make up a tune and sing them, or dance the way they sound. Do you hear any regular patterns of bigger-louder and smaller-softer syllables—maybe every other syllable, or every three syllables?

If you want, scan it! write it down and notate the rhythms. Try putting the pieces of language into groups based on how their rhythms sound to you. Do the groups have anything in common? Do they share a mood, or type of meaning, or tone of voice? How do the different rhythms affect you?

Magical metrical correspondences

Meter is magical. It comes from the same root word as magic, mother, and power (in the proto-Indo-European language).

I consider meter a tool for spiritual and magical work and power, and I have developed over my lifetime a system of analogies and connections between meters and other aspects of life. I am working on a book now that will go into detail about all this!

Meanwhile, you can learn more about these ideas by connecting with me. if you identify as a woman or gender nonconforming, you're welcome to join the Meter Magic Spiral in my website poetrywitchcommunity.org. And people of all genders are invited to join the conversation on my Poetry Witchery blog at anniefinch.substack.com.

ACKNOWLEDGMENTS

Anna Akhmatova (trans. Annie Finch), "Lot's Wife" from *Spells: New and Selected Poems* (Wesleyan University Press, 2013).

Annie Finch, "Samhain" from *Spells: New and Selected Poems* (Wesleyan Press, 2013).

"Kettle Cove" was a commission for *The Voice Was the Sea: Poems from the Maine Coast* by Annie Finch (Voices from the American Land Series, 2012).

"Eve" from *Spells: New and Selected Poems* (Wesleyan Press, 2013).

"Another Reluctance" from *Spells: New and Selected Poems* (Wesleyan Press, 2013).

"Encounter" from *Spells: New and Selected Poems* (Wesleyan Press, 2013).

"My Sister Who Kept Her Abortion A Secret" first appeared in *Tikkun*.

Elizabeth Akers Allen, "Rock Me To Sleep" is in the public domain.

Austin Allen, "There Once Was" first appeared in *Bad Lilies*, Issue 12, February 2023.

Cirilio F. Bautista: (trans. José Edmundo Ocampo Reyes), "Questions and Answers" from *Measure for Measure: An Anthology of Poetic Forms* (Everyman's Library, 2015).

Anna Lena Phillips Bell, "Honeysuckle," *Ornament* (University of North Texas Press, 2017).

Jeffrey Betcher, "Diagnosis," "Wall" and "Mind-Fuck," *Whistling Through* (Poetry Witch Press, 2022).

William Blake, "The Tyger" is in the public domain.

William Stanley Braithwaite, "A Sea-Prayer" is in the public domain.

Elizabeth Barrett Browning, "Sonnet I" from *Sonnets From The Portuguese* is in the public domain.

Paul Laurence Dunbar, "The Paradox" is in the public domain.

Frances Ellen Watkins Harper, "Bury Me In A Free Land" is in the public domain.

Jessie Redmon Fauset, "Rain Fugue" is in the public domain.

Robert Frost, "For Once, Then, Something" is in the public domain.

Thomas Hardy, "The Voice" is in the public domain.

Langston Hughes, "Dream Variations" is in the public domain.

Henry Wadsworth Longfellow, *The Song of Hiawatha* is in the public domain.

John Masefield, "Sea Fever" is in the public domain.

Claude McKay, "If We Must Die" is in the public domain.

Autumn Newman, "Shedding Skin" first appeared in *Pratik: A Magazine of Contemporary Poetry*.

Dorothy Parker, "Fighting Words" is in the public domain.

Edgar Allen Poe, *The Raven* is in the public domain.

Patricia Smith, "The Reemergence of the Noose" first appeared in *Ashville Poetry Review* (2008): 159.

A. E. Stallings, "Arachne Gives Thanks To Athena" first appeared in *Beloit Poetry Journal* 46, no. 2 (Winter 1995-1996).

Sara Teasdale, "I Would Live In Your Love" is in the public domain.

Samuel Woodworth, "The Old Oaken Bucket" is in the public domain.

W. B. Yeats, "When You Are Old" is in the public domain.

www.ingramcontent.com/pod-product-compliance
Lightning Source LLC
Chambersburg PA
CBHW042025100526
44587CB00029B/4295